WHILE MEN SLEPT

CONCORDIA
COLLEGE AND
HIGH SCHOOL

Gift of

T. Teyler

WHILE
MEN SLEPT

by L. Nelson Bell

DOUBLEDAY & COMPANY, INC., GARDEN CITY, NEW YORK
1970

CONTENTS

v

47938

WHAT HAPPENED?

"But while men were sleeping, his enemy came and sowed weeds among the wheat, and went away" (Matthew 13:25).

While men were sleeping the theological seminaries and church-related colleges of America became thoroughly infiltrated with professors who no longer believe in the complete integrity and authority of the written Word of God. Claiming the sanction and support of the many more recently discovered manuscripts, they have been unwilling to admit that not one discovery has invalidated a single cardinal doctrine of the Christian faith. Their rejection of the doctrines clearly stated in the Scriptures stems from philosophical presuppositions which largely rule out the supernatural and the miraculous. In this approach human reason is given precedence over divine revelation.

The destructive critical view of the Bible has become so widespread and is so generally taught and believed in church-related institutions in America that the average student graduating from these schools has had his faith in the full inspiration of the Scriptures either greatly impaired or completely destroyed. This is particularly true in the North, but it is also spreading to the South, although in both areas there are happy exceptions.

As a result, unless they had a thoroughly grounded faith in the Bible *before* entering these institutions, many now go out into Christian work without a vital message. They are forced to substitute reason for faith, reformation for redemption and a program for a Person. The source of power is thought to be in organizations and numbers rather than in the Holy Spirit; and the one weapon designed as the offensive instrument against which Satan has never been able to stand —the Word of the Spirit, the Word of God—has become, in the eyes of these victims of higher critical indoctrination, a largely human and man-made book which must be accepted only in part, with other parts "interpreted" so that its meaning is lost and its power nullified.

It is safe to say that Satan's greatest victory began when he implanted in the minds of Adam and Eve doubt as to the truthfulness of God's Word ("Yea, hath God said?"), and he continues his work today in the classroom of Dr. I. Doubtit, through the writings of Professor W. E. Knowbetter, and from the pulpit of Dr. Will Knott Believe.

There is a question as to just how far rationalistic unbelief has infiltrated theological thinking and teaching today. Certainly the great majority of Christian leaders believe most of the great doctrines of the Church, but apparently an increasing number have had their confidence in the Bible so greatly shaken that they hold impaired views with reference to truths which are a part of the Christian faith and without which all teaching and preaching is lacking in transforming power.

Held in question are doctrines having to do with the reality of sin, eternal punishment, the personality of Satan and the efficacy of prayer. The God of the Old Testament, we are told, is not the same God found in the New Testament. Many affirm belief in the deity of our Lord who at the same time question His virgin birth, the reality of His miracles, His vicarious atonement for our sins on Calvary, His bodily resurrection, and the reality of His eventual return in power and glory. True, few would question or deny all of these doctrines, but many have doubts about one or more of them, although all are clearly taught in God's Word and are a part of most evangelical creeds.

We ask where this unbelief has come from and why it is so widespread today. *Protestant Christendom has been asleep and during our sleep the enemy of souls, under the guise of scholarship and advanced knowledge, has sown the seeds of doubt and unbelief.* Tolerance—tolerance to error—has been the watchword. The feelings and positions of teachers have been more sympathetically regarded than have the victims of the insidious sowing of seeds of unbelief. Some who hold the evangelical faith have fought back with the weapons of hate and with half-truths and have only complicated the situation. Others have been utterly indifferent to the tragic results of unbelief being caught in church-related institutions —apparently with the hope that the name "Christian" offers some magic which may overrule and sublimate teachings which are utterly inimical to that faith.

Is there a solution? Is there a way out? Of course there is, but it must be undergirded with prayer and executed in love. The ruthless extirpation of tares has always harmed the wheat. Any zeal for the Lord which does not combine with it Christian love, holy boldness and sanctified common sense, is destined to add to the confusion.

The solution must be based on a standard, and that standard depends for its authority on God and His revealed truth. While there are those who object to such authority, it is nevertheless axiomatic that for everything there must be

ix

laws—the rules of the game. To undertake to live in the Christian realm one must accept the basis of Christianity or automatically disqualify himself. It is here that many have disqualified themselves in the theological world, for they deny the validity of the Standard which God has given, lowering it to a more or less man-made document. *Reason* is given the throne which rightfully belongs only to *faith*.

In the Presbyterian Church, the Confession of Faith states the basis of our authority in these words: "The authority of the Holy Scripture, for which it ought to be believed and obeyed, dependeth not upon the testimony of any man or church, but wholly upon God (who is truth itself), the author thereof; and therefore it is to be received, because it is the Word of God." (Ch. I, section IV); while section VIII goes on to say: "The Old Testament in Hebrew, and the New Testament in Greek, being immediately inspired by God, and by his singular care and providence kept pure in all ages, are therefore authentical; so as in all controversies of religion the church is finally to appeal to them."

Most of the other evangelical churches have in their articles of faith equally clear affirmations as to the reliability and authority of God's Word. But in many of the church-related institutions in Protestant circles today these statements regarding the Word of God are being disregarded or explained away. Apparently Protestantism is more concerned with ecclesiastical organization, power and prestige than with the touchy questions having to do with the basic facts of the Christian faith itself.

When attention is called to these deviations from evangelical Christianity, a barrage of most unpleasant opprobrium is heaped on the individual who has the temerity to do so, and if possible ecclesiastical pressures are exerted on him. He is called "divisive" and a "Dispensationalist"—although he may reject this particular deviation from Christian teaching as completely as the rest. He is accused of being a "fundamentalist"—although he too may deplore the loveless-ness of the professional Fundamentalist (capital "F")—as much as any; and of being more concerned about a book than a Person, even though his concern is for the honesty of the Book which tells about *the* Person. Such browbeating is not easy to take and many remain silent hoping the tide will turn. Others are silent because their livelihood is at stake. But unless there is a concerted stand, Protestant power and witness in America is doomed, except as the torch is taken up by lesser denominations and by sects—an eventuality many would regret, because of the extreme positions and bizarre doctrines held by some of these and which have little or nothing to do with the essential truths of Christianity.

To make fun of the plenary inspiration of the Scriptures is so common and so popular today that few will have the temerity to stand against this tide of unbelief. However, whenever one pins down the adherents of this modern schol-arship, he finds the same objections to the Bible which have been raised and answered for centuries. *There is nothing new* in the present-day denials, and this makes them obsolete and unworthy of continued exploitation.

It would seem only fair that those who no longer hold to the integrity of the Scriptures should dissociate themselves with the evangelical denominations that hold such beliefs and that have them incorporated in their articles of faith. One can but respect the honesty of men who so make their belief—or unbelief—a matter of record. At the same time one wonders at the theological schizophrenia that permits a man to subscribe to vows with a mental reservation or an interpre-tation totally at variance with their accepted meaning. As an illustration: a prominent clergyman recently affirmed his acceptance of the "theological implications" of the Virgin Birth, but questioned "the biological fact." Another, decrying the preaching of the necessity of the new birth, stated categorically, "I am not a sinner."

We have the conviction that when laymen in the United States become aware of the unbelief which is being taught in many church-related institutions under the guise of scholarship and advanced scientific knowledge—particularly the blatant denial of great portions of the Bible and of doctrines clearly stated therein—they will in increasing numbers, rise up and ask for an accounting of stewardship.

In 1953, Dr. Rozenkrantz of New York University, speaking of a survey he had just completed for the (then) U. S. A. Presbyterian Church, said that he could observe no difference between their colleges and the secular state universities. About that same time, a well-known bishop of the Episcopal Church called the clergymen in his diocese together and frankly told them they were neither teaching nor preaching the doctrines affirmed in their own articles of faith. Identical conditions are to be found in *all* of the major denominations.

What has happened? While Protestant Christians have been asleep, the enemy has done a thorough job of sowing the seeds of unbelief.

What can we do? We can and must pray for a heaven-sent revival of faith in God and in His Word. Although many will deny it, *THEY GO TOGETHER.*

WHILE MEN SLEPT

Because of what happened—WE SEE . . .

UNREST IN THE CHURCH

For entirely too long church leaders ignored the growing unrest within the churches. Often it seemed they were trying to sweep the fact under the rug of frenetic programs and activity. Usually they blamed the unrest on those who protested its causes.

No longer can this unrest be ignored. There are now too many dedicated Christians raising their voices in protest. They see through the pleas for "relevancy" to a subtle change in basic emphases they cannot accept. They know something of what the Church should stand for and what it should do, and have the courage to stand up and speak against what they honestly feel to be a perversion of the Church, both in message and in activity.

This unrest is now noted by secular publications. The March *Ladies Home Journal* carries a survey of what 1,000 women had to say about the Church under the startling heading, "You Can't Find God in the Church Anymore!"

To this, however, I should like to be the first to reply that obviously these women, and several million more unfortunates like them, have been going to the wrong churches. There are tens of thousands of churches where God is to be found,

1

where his Son and his Gospel are believed and preached, and where the Written Word of God is given top priority, in matters of faith and of daily living.

But it is tragically true that most of the major denominations are now dominated by men who have shifted the emphasis of the Church and, in so doing, are neglecting the message of belief in Christ as man's Saviour from sin which is the first step toward a right relationship with God.

The scientific approach to problem-solving is to go back and find the source of the problem and then try to remedy it. What is the source of unrest in the Church? Besides the almost inevitable clashes of personalities, what lies at the root of this problem that is tearing the churches apart?

I write as one layman who has been concerned with this matter for many years, not with the feeling that I know all the answers, but with the assurance that the things I am trying to point out have much to do with the problem.

The mainstream of Protestantism has been polluted by theologians who have willfully rejected faith in the complete integrity and authority of the Word of God. *This lies at the source of all that has followed.*

Part of the problem is "scholarship"—not genuine scholarship with its reverent search for truth, but an arrogant intellectualism against which the Apostle Paul warned Timothy ("Avoid the godless mixture of contradictory notions which is falsely known as 'knowledge'—some have followed it and lost their faith," I Tim. 6:20, 21, Phillips). This attitude gives the opinions of men precedence over the divine revelation. It has dominated the majority of the theological seminaries of Europe and America until today a new religion has emerged that is humanism, not Christianity.

The evidences of theological laxity are all about us. Christ is portrayed as a good man who did the work of an idealistic

2

humanitarian. As for the Bible, many of its records are regarded as the accounts of overly enthusiastic followers of our Lord. The Old Testament, together with much of the New, is considered outmoded and no longer relevant for our sophisticated age.

Out of this rejection of the Scriptures have grown some devastating theories. One is that there are no longer absolutes; everything is relative. (This statement is itself expressed as an absolute, of course.) How can the holiness of God be relative? He is pure and good. Can his truth be subordinated to man's sinful outlook?

This does not deter some modern church leaders from making morality relative, to the point where fornication and adultery are judged, not by God's holy law, but according to the "love" and immediate circumstances of the two persons involved. I am convinced that the new morality, or situation ethics, fits into Paul's warning, "Now the Spirit expressly says that in later times some will depart from the faith by giving heed to deceitful spirits and doctrines of demons, through the pretensions of liars whose consciences are seared" (I Tim. 4:1, 2).

The average person attends church to hear messages that speak to his spirit. He may be frustrated and uncertain, longing for spiritual light. Tragically, he may hear no more than a sociological discourse, an appeal to "go out and do something," with no reference to the One who came and died and rose again so that men might truly live.

There is unrest in the Church, not only because of the changed view of Jesus Christ, but also because of the new approach to the problems of man. The emphasis is not on man's sin and his need of a Saviour; it is on his physical, political, and economic environment. Thank God many Christians are refusing to take this lying down.

The social implications of Christianity are very real, and the Christian *is* to be his brother's keeper. But the Church,

3

as such, is not an organization for social engineering. Its primary concern is not with the social order but with the individual souls that need Christ.

Unrest in the Church? Thank God for it! When a patient is insensitive to pain he is in a critical condition. The healthy human body will usually reject poison; a sick one may permit it to do its deadly work without reacting. The current discontent is a sign that there are thousands of Christians who know the difference between true Christianity and a deadening substitute.

Perhaps it is natural that many who control the machinery of the Church blame "dissidents" for the situation, and that, where they can, they work to silence these dissenting voices. (And we might add that they are sometimes ruthless in their efforts to suppress and punish.)

What is the solution? Perhaps above all else we need a renewed emphasis on the Holy Spirit, a realization that without his presence and power, all work of the Church is futile. Where he is given his rightful place, there is a spiritual awakening and revival, and a new appreciation of the Word of God as the Sword of the Spirit. When it is acknowledged that, far from being obsolete or irrelevant, the Bible is the most relevant book of all, then the Christ portrayed therein and the Gospel concerning him are preached with conviction and power.

Unrest in the Church? Thank God for this evidence of life! Thank God that people are taking heed to the warning: "Hear, O earth; behold I am bringing evil upon this people, the fruit of their devices, because they have not given heed to my words; and as for my law, they have rejected it" (Jer. 6:19).

Part of the trouble is because of . . .

MISSION ABORTED

If the church has as its chief mission the witnessing to the saving power of Jesus Christ, then it should certainly be more concerned with this business than it now seems to be. If, on the other hand, its chief mission is to transform society through social engineering, then it is being increasingly diligent in its calling—but woefully ineffective.

Is the Church in the world to conquer the world for righteousness? Or is it in the world to bear testimony that Jesus Christ, God's Son, has opened the way to God by his death and resurrection? Is the Church supposed to be a *conquering organization* or a *witnessing organism?* The way that question is answered determines the course of the Church and its success or failure in the eyes of God.

The idea of the Church may easily be perverted so that it becomes the agency through which man, not God, works. It is to this danger that I speak.

Analysis of many of the major concerns and activities of the church today leads to this somber conclusion: Even if every objective were to be realized, unless at the same time there were added the spiritual dimension of the Gospel's

5

call to individuals to repent of their sins and accept Jesus as Saviour and Lord, the world would still be populated with lost souls.

The Church's giving top priority to the secular and material problems of mankind can only mean that there are those in places of leadership who have lost, or never had, a realization of man's desperate spiritual needs.

This is not an appeal to preserve the status quo. It is not an attempt to project "seventeenth-century theology into the twentieth." And it is not a conviction based on an insensitivity to the dire needs of people living in an advanced technological age, or on lack of concern for the pressing social problems of poverty, discrimination, and the inequities that produce internal strife and external warfare.

In looking over the catalogues of major theological seminaries, one notes that, with few exceptions, theological education today majors on the world's secular and material ills. This being true, who will train men to speak to the spiritual needs of mankind? Into this vacuum of theological training either new or truly converted institutions will arise. Man does *not* live by bread alone, though some seem to think so. Man *can* gain all the world has to offer and still lose his soul. And when the Kingdom of God and his righteousness are put *first,* then material needs are mysteriously met. Shall we allow the people of this generation to join with David in saying, "No man cared for my soul" (Ps. 142:4b)?

I am *not* discounting the fact of desperate human need and the necessity that every Christian play the role of the Samaritan. We need to pray earnestly for greater compassion and love and an ever increasing sensitivity to the plight of the needy, wherever they may be found. But I am pleading for the Church and the individual Christian to endeavor to see in those we try to serve *souls for whom Christ died.*

I am concerned about this matter because I see "social

6

concern" being used as a substitute for the Gospel of redemption. I see many operating within the context of the Church who no longer accept the biblical doctrine of man and sin, who no longer proclaim the Bible-revealed Son of God as man's one hope of forgiveness and spiritual healing. Because I see social engineering replacing the preaching of the simple Gospel, I am concerned for the Church lest it find "Ichabod" written across its portals.

Take as an example the problem of grinding poverty. Let us grant, first, that "affluence" and "poverty" are relative terms, and, second, that the Christian is responsible for implementing his faith with works of generosity and compassion; still the fact remains that while immediate need must be met by immediate action, the *long-range solution*, which it is the Church's obligation to preach, is that when God is put first in our lives we have the word of our Lord that material sufficiency follows.

By exalting Christ as the answer to man's greatest need, and his promises as man's greatest asset, the Church would ultimately do far more to alleviate poverty than a dozen governmental programs.

Furthermore, through the centuries the church has performed its mightiest service to society as a whole when, working in the power of the Spirit, it has led men to Jesus Christ and turned them loose on the world. By neglecting its calling to give top priority to the things of the spirit, it becomes derelict in its duty and vulnerable to the siren calls of a godless society.

In meeting immediate need, wherever it may be found (which is the Christian's duty), the Church has no right to claim for an unbelieving world those benefits that God has promised solely to those who put him first in their lives.

7

Nor has it a mandate to enlist the government to carry out what it considers to be its obligations to society.

Today we see church agencies contributing to secular projects such as low-cost housing, poverty programs, civil-rights movements, and the like. It is one thing if the allocated funds were given for such projects; it is quite another if they come from budgets raised to preach the Gospel at home or abroad.

Acutely aware of a social order out of kilter, the Church is in grave danger of failing to rise to its God-ordained task of seeking to make new creatures in Christ. It is new hearts that men need, and it is men with new hearts who alone can change the desperate conditions of our day.

The process of conversion one by one seems too slow to many. But it is God's way, and he has offered to the Church the power of the Gospel, the power of the Cross, the power of a resurrected Christ, and the power of his Spirit.

Can man find a better way?

Let's be frank—

to maintain the truth there must be . . .

CONTROVERSY

Controversy is always unpleasant, and most people shrink from the prospect of becoming involved in it. Disagreements and disputes bring anguish of mind. In the Church, controversy has caused unhappiness and divisions, so much so that many say they will have no part in anything controversial.

Nevertheless, error that is propagated in the name of truth must be resisted.

Pain and inflammation are nature's warning of infection in the body. So it is with the Church. Where error is presented as truth, evil as good, man as sovereign above God, there must be a reaction, and this reaction means controversy. Only by such reactions is it possible for the Church to maintain purity of doctrine and life.

When a body no longer reacts to harmful stimuli, it is either desperately sick or dead. The same is true of the Church.

Unfortunately, there have always been disagreements over secondary matters. Some have been the result of personality clashes in which bruised human egos triumphed over what should have been Christian humility.

But where there are deviations from basic Christian truths, there must be reactions for the truth. Such reactions are good and right and are a blessing to the Church as a whole.

Obviously there must be a source of reference, a norm on which to base convictions. This is found in the Holy Scriptures.

The New Testament gives abundant proof that our Lord and the founders of the early Church harked back to the Old Testament as the basis of their authority. They accepted at face value statements that some today would say were "taken out of context" but that were really messages of the Holy Spirit received by those whose minds and hearts were open to his teaching.

In subsequent church history, the early fathers went to the Word of God for guidance and authority. Later years brought the Westminster Confession of Faith, produced by a group of about 150 men who were noted for their deep and reverent scholarship and who worked five days a week for over five years. This monumental work, which has never been excelled as a statement of the Christian faith and the reasons for it, says this about the Scriptures: "The authority of the Holy Scriptures, for which it ought to be believed and obeyed, dependeth not upon the testimony of any man or church, but wholly upon God (who is truth itself), the author thereof; and therefore it is to be received, because it is the word of God" (chap. 1:IV).

Section V continues: "We may be moved and induced by the testimony of the church to a high and reverent esteem for the Holy Scripture; and the heavenliness of the matter, the efficacy of the doctrine, the majesty of the style, the consent of all the parts, the scope of the whole (which is to give all glory to God), the full discovery it makes of the only way of man's salvation, the many other incomparable

1

excellencies, and the entire perfection thereof, are arguments whereby it doth evidence itself to be the word of God; yet, notwithstanding, our full persuasion and assurance of the infallible truth and divine authority thereof, is from the inward work of the Holy Spirit, bearing witness by and with the word in our hearts."

Somewhat quaintly worded, yes; I have no unyielding attachment to his particular wording. But I know of no finer statement of the complete integrity and authority of the Holy Scriptures.

The most important thing to remember in dealing with the matter of Christian controversy is that it is not what men think or say but what the Scriptures say that is of ultimate significance.

In the early Church, Judaizers went up to Antioch and troubled the Gentile Christians by telling them that circumcision was necessary for salvation. The future of the Church was at stake. Was salvation a work of God's free grace to be received by faith alone, or were there other requirements? Was the Christian under the bondage of the Law, or was he freed from that bondage by Christ?

If one reads Paul's letter to the Galatian Christians in conjunction with Luke's account of the meeting in Jerusalem, one realizes that Paul attended the meeting, not to receive instructions, but to tell of God's work of grace among the Gentiles and of his own clear, direct revelation from Jesus Christ. Paul entered into this controversy with convictions nothing could shake. He knew that a deadly heresy was being injected into the life of the Church, and he would not tolerate it.

Matters brought to court must be resolved by reference to applicable laws. To act in defiance of the clear meaning of the law brings chaos and anarchy.

In differences within the Church, the final decisions must be made in accordance with the clear teachings of the Scriptures. Like the Bereans who, when they heard the Apostle Paul, searched the Scriptures to see whether his preaching was true, the Church must take the Bible as the final authority. If it does not, the way is opened for any heresy.

When controversy takes place in a spirit of Christian love, all can benefit. It is lack of love that brings discredit. Paul warns those who find it necessary to oppose a disobedient person not to "look on him as an enemy but to warn him as a brother" (II Thess. 3:15). But for those who would preach "another gospel," Paul has only the severest condemnation (Gal. 1:8, 9).

Controversy demands not only love but also humility, a humility that is willing to take rebuffs, unjust criticism, and misunderstanding, all for the glory and honor of God. Once we let personalities prevail, the battle is lost and our witness for good vanishes.

Let us also beware of gloating over the sin of others and broadcasting it to the world. There is no surer way to lose one's testimony for the right.

Controversy is necessary when the truth is perverted or assailed. But we must beware lest our contending for the faith become contentiousness, accompanied by bitterness, lovelessness, and harshness of judgment.

The whole question of truth has to do with God and his revelation to man. It has to do with the person and work of Jesus Christ and the record we have of him in both the Old and the New Testament. It has to do with doctrines and their application to our own lives.

To speak out in defense of the Christian faith is serious business, and it is difficult to do with grace and humility;

but it is not sinful. To remain silent when the faith is perverted or denied *is* sinful. If there is danger of disturbing the peace of the Church by speaking, there is far more danger when the purity of the Church is threatened and no one speaks.

Controversy there must be, when the purity of the Church is in danger; but it should be carried on in an atmosphere of prayer, Christian love, and dependence upon the help of the Holy Spirit.

*One of our serious problems is that
only too often the
Church leadership has connived in . . .*

CIVIL DISOBEDIENCE

Calculated civil disobedience, seemingly so innocent, has brought in an era of lawlessness and bloodshed that can plunge our nation into unbelievable chaos. The tragic death of Dr. Martin Luther King, Jr., and subsequent events bear mute testimony to the uncontrolled forces now unloosed across the land.

In recent years nearly every major denomination has passed resolutions on civil disobedience defending the principle of resistance to the law and constituted authority while admitting that those who break the law must be prepared to accept the consequences.

What a few years ago appeared to be a gesture of sympathy toward those engaged in civil disobedience has now developed into support of individuals and movements that are challenging constitutional procedures and encouraging a spirit of rebellion and anarchy. Some churchmen now say openly that there must be revolution, even bloodshed, before there can be a new social order.

Perhaps this year will prove to be the last chance for general assemblies, conferences, conventions, and the like to take a second look at a philosophy that is able to destroy the foundations of the nation. For if lawlessness prevails, the outlook for America is bleak. Civil disobedience can lead to the dissolution of law and order, with anarchy the result. Further, it can lead to revolution. And revolution can open the way to dictatorship, with the resulting loss of freedom and ultimate bondage.

Riots, bloodshed, arson, loss of life and property—a dismal story—are the result of trying to redress wrongs in the streets rather than in the courts and at the ballot box. In rejecting "gradualism" with its attending frustrations and disappointments, many are resorting to a senseless rebellion that adds tensions and injustice.

Writing in *Look* magazine under the title, "Dissent or Destruction?," Eric Sevareid observed:

"The use of force to express conviction, even if it takes so relatively mild a form as a college sit-in that blocks the administration building, is intolerable. When Dr. Martin Luther King, who may well be one of the noblest Americans of the century, deliberately defies a court order, then he ought to go to jail. Laws and ordinances can be changed, and are constantly being changed, but they cannot be rewritten in the streets where other citizens also have their rights" (*Look*, Sept. 5, 1967, pp. 22, 23; copyright 1967 by Eric Sevareid; used by permission).

To engage in or condone civil disobedience is to loose a tiger of destruction. The welfare of any nation depends on respect for and enforcement of law. Lawlessness is now prevalent enough to endanger the very life of our nation. Laws that are inadequate or unjust should be changed in the courts and at the polls; they cannot be changed in the streets.

Furthermore, those who incite riots and disorder, who advocate violent disruption of communities and go about as

15

hatemongers, whether they be members of secret organizations like the Ku Klux Klan, black-power advocates, or something else, should be handled by the law on the basis of their public threats, before they commit violent acts.

Any person who openly flouts the law should be called to account.

The hooded organization that engages in terrorism, arson, and bombings should be infiltrated by representatives of the law until its leaders are behind bars and its members scattered into oblivion.

The wave of civil disobedience that is threatening our national life seems to have paralyzed us into fear and inaction. But unless it is reversed, we face anarchy. No segment of society can be permitted to act above the law and to destroy the things on which a decent society is based.

We are on the verge of being frightened enough to believe that the outlay of hundreds of billions of dollars is the answer to our problem. No one questions the need to rebuild our cities; but chaos cannot be cured by money, no matter how great the sum. Even if every person in America were put in a mansion, without regard for law and order our problem would continue.

No one can deny that we have countenanced discrimination and humiliation to such a point that a sense of frustration is inevitable; now this frustration has caused violent reactions. These sins against human beings must cease, and equal opportunities must be available to all. But with these needed changes (and tremendous progress is being made in this direction), respect for law and law enforcement must be maintained.

This is no plea for maintaining the status quo. It is a plea for recognition that the blindness and unconcern of the dominant segment of our society must be completely changed. And on the other hand, it is an affirmation that any status

16

and rights gained through civil disorder will be gained at too high a price.

Two centuries ago Edmund Burke, the great English statesman, gave this warning: "Men are qualified for civil liberties in exact proportion to their disposition to put moral chains upon their own appetites. . . . Society cannot exist unless a controlling power upon will and appetite is placed somewhere, and the less of it there is within, the more there must be without. It is ordained in the eternal constitution of things that men of intemperate minds cannot be free. Their passions forge their fetters."

In medicine there is a condition known as "generalized carcinomatosis," which, in layman's language, means cancer that has spread over the entire body. At that stage there is no known cure.

The lawlessness that has entered our national life through civil disobedience—a concept having the approval of most of the major denominations—can prove to be the moral cancer that will destroy our country.

This is a plea to churchmen to take stock of what has been loosed upon the land. Civil disobedience is not the "harmless gesture of protest" it was once said to be. Rather, it has grown into a monster of disorder, riots, and general lawlessness that is eating at the vitals of our national life. It is proving as senseless—and as devastating—as the proverbial "burning down the barn to get rid of the rats."

Some of our most distinguished jurists and law-makers have deplored the actions of various church courts in condoning civil disobedience. Sufficient time has now elapsed to assess the damage; one has but to open his daily newspaper to realize that we totter on the brink of open rebellion.

Responsible law-makers must do everything they can to

17

eliminate injustice, discrimination, and humiliation. At the same time, those who administer the law must be supported at all costs.

The alternative is national disaster.

In fact, we are face to face with . . .

THE GREAT COUNTERFEIT

Many years ago I saw one of the world's greatest magicians perform some amazing feats of legerdemain. If we in the audience had not known we were being deceived, we would all have believed he had supernatural powers. Through his swiftness of hand, practiced diverting of the audience's attention, and use of prepared props and equipment, the magician gave us a good show, both amusing and instructive.

Today, within the bounds of the Church, we are witnessing a Satanic work of deception and substitution that is intended to deceive even the very elect. This giant hoax is *the substitution of humanism for Christianity.*

The welfare of man is a worthy objective. But when that welfare becomes an end in itself, with no reference to man's eternal soul, it is high time for Christians to take a look.

Humanism's concern is for material values, but Christianity places spiritual values above all else.

Humanism is concerned with *now,* with time and all that occurs in the present. Christianity's eyes are set on eternity, on the city made without hands, eternal in the heavens.

For the humanist, the "gospel" had to do with man's reconciliation to man; but Christianity's Gospel puts man's reconciliation to God through Jesus Christ above all else.

The humanist sees "sin" as primarily man's maladjustment to man; for the Christian, sin is disobedience to God's revealed will.

Humanism is concerned about man's physical, environmental, emotional, and material welfare, but not about his soul. Christianity recognizes that only as man is reconciled to God can he be properly adjusted to the conditions of everyday life, and that by the presence and grace of God situations that otherwise would be unbearable are often means to draw him closer to God.

Humanism is willing to make use of any secular power or means to accomplish its ends. Christianity depends on the presence and power of the Holy Spirit for its effectiveness.

Christians need to recognize the solemn fact that humanism is not an ally in making the world a better place in which to live. It is a deadly enemy for it is a religion without God and without hope in this world or the next.

The danger lies in the confusion of the objectives of humanism and Christianity, a confusion rooted in totally divergent concepts of God and man.

In 1933 a group of humanists convened and prepared a manifesto. This was signed by thirty-four of their leaders, twelve of whom were prominent ministers. The manifesto was as follows:

"*First:* Religious humanists regard the universe as self-existing and not created.

"*Second:* Humanism believes that man is a part of nature and that he has emerged as the result of a continuous process.

"*Third:* Holding an organic view of life, humanists find that traditional dualism of mind and body must be rejected.

"*Fourth:* Humanism recognizes that man's religious culture and civilization, as clearly depicted by anthropology and history, are the product of a gradual development due to his interaction with his natural environment and with his social heritage. . . .

"*Fifth:* Humanism asserts that the nature of the universe depicted by modern science makes unacceptable any supernatural or cosmic guarantees of human values. . . . Religion must formulate its hopes and plans in the light of the scientific spirit and method.

"*Sixth:* We are convinced that the time has passed for theism, deism, modernism, and the several varieties of 'new thought.'

"*Seventh:* Religion consists of those actions, purposes, and experiences which are humanly significant. Nothing human is alien to the religious. It includes labor, art, science, philosophy, love, friendship, recreation—all that is in its degree expressive of intelligently satisfying human living. The distinction between the sacred and the secular can no longer be maintained.

"*Eighth:* Religious humanism considers the complete realization of human personality to be the end of man's life and seeks its development and fulfillment in the here and now. This is the explanation of the humanist's social passion.

"*Ninth:* In place of the old attitudes involved in worship and prayer the humanist finds his religious emotions expressed in a heightened sense of personal life and in a cooperative effort to promote social well-being.

"*Tenth:* It follows that there will be no uniquely religious emotions and attitudes of the kind hitherto associated with belief in the supernatural.

"*Eleventh:* Man will learn to face the crises of life in terms of his knowledge of their naturalness and probability. Reasonable and manly attitudes will be fostered by education and supported by custom. We assume that humanism will take the path of social and mental hygiene and discourage sentimental and unreal hopes and wishful thinking.

"Twelfth: Believing that religion must work increasingly for joy in living, religious humanists aim to foster the creative in man and to encourage achievements that add to the satisfactions of life.

"Thirteenth: Religious humanism maintains that all associations and institutions exist for the fulfillment of human life. . . . Certainly religious institutions, their ritualistic forms, ecclesiastical methods, and communal activities must be reconstituted as rapidly as experience allows, in order to function effectively in the modern world.

Fourteenth: The humanists are firmly convinced that existing acquisitive and profit-motivated society has shown itself inadequate and that radical change in methods, controls, and motives must be instituted. A socialized and cooperative economic order must be established to the end that equitable distribution of the means of life is possible. The goal of humanism is a free and universal society in which people voluntarily and intelligently cooperate for the common good. Humanists demand a shared life in a shared world.

"Fifteenth and last: We assert that humanism will: (a) affirm life rather than deny it; (b) seek to elicit the possibilities of life, not flee from it; and (c) endeavor to establish the conditions of a satisfactory life for all, not merely the few. By this positive morale and intention humanism will be guided, and from this perspective and alignment the techniques and efforts of humanism will flow."

This manifesto is a frank statement of the great counterfeit being perpetrated on today's world, one for which many within the Church have fallen.

Play down the fact of sin in the human heart; think of

man as sufficient in himself; obliterate God and his Christ from their sovereign rights—then you have humanism as a substitute for Christianity, and man's efforts in the place of redemption through Christ.

Humanism, the supreme counterfeit, is here among us. Recognize it and turn from it as you would turn from the plague. Our hope is in Christ and in nothing else.

Little wonder that we see . . .

LAY CONCERN

In almost every major denomination today laymen are showing more and more concern over the lessening of emphasis on the spiritual nature and message of the Church.

Church leaders have always solicited the interest and support of laymen. Some are now finding that many laymen have become restive about some programs they are being asked to support. Many feel their leaders are promoting activities outside the province of the Church, placing primary emphasis on secondary things, and seeking to reform society without the redemption of individuals.

Recently members of a Southern Presbyterian lay organization known as Concerned Presbyterians (address: 234 Biscayne Boulevard, Miami, Florida) met with members of another group within the denomination that represents a more liberal approach to the mission of the Church, particularly in the area of social action. The meeting was called by the moderator of the church.

Some ministers present expressed deep apprehension because Concerned Presbyterians is made up entirely of laymen. In reply the president of that group said frankly that this was necessary because ministers who joined might be subject to "ecclesiastical reprisals." But a number of ministers are quietly helping the organization.

For about two years there has existed in the United Presbyterian Church a group called the Presbyterian Lay Committee, whose board is composed of some of America's most distinguished Christian laymen and churchmen. In January this group (offices at 200 Fifth Avenue, New York City) began publishing a monthly magazine called *The Presbyterian Layman,* "edited for the entire membership of the United Presbyterian Church." It is a "voice of the laity, expected to stimulate greater discussion in Church matters, foster constructive ideas for strengthening the United Presbyterian Church, encourage more dedicated involvement of laymen and women in the activities of their own churches, and also to encourage laymen to take public positions as Christian citizens on secular matters."

This group, when questioned about its position ("Is it conservative or liberal? Is it fundamental, traditional or modern? Reactionary or progressive? Right or left? Capitalistic or socialistic? Existentialistic or antidisestablishmentarianistic?"), replied that it "rejects all labels" and "intends to conduct its affairs guided by the Scriptures, as clearly defined in the Westminster Confession of Faith."

This unrest is not confined to one denomination. Groups of laymen in every major denomination are becoming concerned and are expressing their concern with growing vigor. This is being demonstrated in the Methodist Church while some of the most vigorous lay movements are found among Episcopalians. The unrest is noted in both the Southern Baptist Convention and in the American Baptist Convention. In fact, the bright spot in the general situation throughout Protestantism is that laymen in increasing numbers are leading

25

movements back to the historical faith and away from a watered-down and secularized religion.

It is hoped that the too-violent reactions of some laymen will be calmed down by others, and there is evidence this is now taking place. Because of the mushrooming of these lay movements and the spiritual awakening they are bringing in their wake, they need careful evaluation. There are many who feel strongly that the hope of the Church now rests with aroused and dedicated laymen.

Here are some of the reasons for concern cited by many laymen:

• The preaching they too often hear, stressing some form of social action or activity without a corresponding emphasis on the redemptive work of Christ at the personal level;

• The institutional church's participation in pronouncements on almost any subject, its taking of positions on controversial matters without either the mandate or the competence to do so;

• A growing tendency to enlist the political and economic power of the federal government on behalf of schemes dear to church leaders that, almost without exception, point straight to the concepts of a socialistic state—despite the ever-increasing evidence of the failure of socialism wherever practiced;

• A shift in emphasis from the individual to society as a whole, though the primary aim of the Gospel is to reach individual persons, and through them the social structure.

• A shift in emphasis from distinctively Christian programs to basically humanistic ones ("there seems more concern that the surroundings of the Prodigal, and his personal comfort, shall be improved rather than that he shall be called back to his Father in penitence and restitution");

• A new and false interpretation of "evangelism" in terms of social engineering and revolution rather than proclamation of the redeeming love and grace of God in the person and work of his Son;

• A preoccupation with this world and its ills without a corresponding concern for the souls of sinners who desperately need the Saviour;

• A failure of many church leaders to take the Bible seriously, with the result that they are tossed to and fro on the seas of human speculation without the anchor of a clear "Thus saith the Lord";

• The implicit redefining of the good and proper word "ecumenical" to mean "organizational." Little of the true spirit of ecumenicity is offered to evangelicals and distinctly evangelical organizations such as Campus Crusade and Inter-Varsity.

These lay movements are not schismatic. By and large members recognize that an effective witness can be borne only *within* the denominations; splitting only adds to the problems. These laymen are true loyalists—loyal to their churches and to the standards that are part of their heritage.

This is not nostalgia for the past. Those who are concerned know well that neither the Church nor the world can be turned back. They *are* nostalgic for a renewed realization that the Gospel of Jesus Christ is relevant for the needs of every age and that, by the power of the Holy Spirit, it can bring about a marvelous change in men and nations today, just as it did in the first Christian century. (One detractor said about some of these laymen in the South, "They would like to go back a hundred years and wave the Confederate flag." One wonders what flag their Northern counterparts would presumably like to wave. The Union Jack?)

These movements are not a call for maintaining the status quo; some of these laymen seem far more aware of the world and its basic needs than the social activists.

27

Nor are they an attempt to drive a wedge between the pulpit and the pew. While there are undoubtedly laymen who resist all change and who also have their social consciousness blurred by bigotry, prejudice, and pride, the laymen who are furthering these movements are concerned with personal obedience to their Lord and loyalty to their church. Their goal is to see that the Church continues as a spiritual power and does not degenerate into an organization with social action as its primary concern. If this concern is divisive, it is others who must assume the blame.

The world is in a desperate plight. One social activist recently said, "The world is going to hell while we nit-pick." But these laymen are *not* "nit-picking." Tens of thousands of persons believe that the plight of men and nations is not beyond the redeeming and transforming power of the Lord Jesus Christ. They do not want him crowded out by a program of social engineering. They believe the task is a personal one, winning *individual* men to Christ. Then and only then can "society be redeemed."

*In trying to be "relevant" we should go
back to our source and ask
ourselves how we could compare . . .*

THEN AND NOW

Comparisons can be invidious. They can also be instructive
and profitable. For instance, a comparison of the physician
Luke with the physicians of today reveals the tremendous
strides made in medicine during the past 2,000 years.

This is no reflection on Luke. I am sure that a man who
was such a careful historian was equally conscientious in
the practice of his profession. His character was unblemished,
and his dedicated personality led the Apostle Paul to speak
of him as "Luke the beloved physician."

But since Luke's time and particularly in the last few
decades, the practice of medicine and surgery has been revolutionized. What is commonplace today would have been
unbelievable even a few years ago.

Visiting in one of our great medical centers, I watched
a friend, a much younger surgeon, perform what is now
a routine operation in many hospitals. He removed most of
the abdominal aorta (for a large aneurysm) and the two
large arteries leading down through the pelvis, replacing
them with a plastic counterpart in and through which a new
aorta and branches would develop. The care, precision, and

lack of haste of the surgeon and his three assistants bore testimony to their training and skill. And, best of all, the patient made a brilliant recovery.

As for the new medicines, it is said that 90 per cent of the prescriptions now written by physicians are for medicines not in use even ten years ago.

It is obvious that while the character of Luke the physician has not been improved upon, the practice of medicine and surgery has advanced fantastically. Bodily ailments continue as in Luke's day, but the means of relief are immeasurably improved.

What about the preaching of Peter and Paul? How does it compare with preaching today? Luke's profession sought to heal sickness of the body. Peter and Paul preached to bring healing to the souls of men.

While the practice of medicine has advanced since Luke's day to unthought-of heights, much of present-day preaching has *regressed*. This is not meant to be a universal judgment, of course. Yet the facts cannot be ignored.

The preaching of Peter and Paul was based on an accurate spiritual diagnosis and the offer of a sure cure. Much preaching today *evades* the basic sickness of the soul and prescribes nostrums no more effective than the incantations of a witch doctor.

Those early apostles confronted their hearers with the fact of sin, its enormity, its wages, and its cure. They preached sin, judgment, repentance, and forgiveness through the atoning work and shed blood of Calvary, and they got results.

They made use of the power available in their time and equally so today—the power of the Holy Spirit, the power of the Scriptures, and the power of prayer. How much preaching today is dependent on the power of the Holy Spirit to make it effective, the power of the Scriptures as the Sword of the

Spirit, and the power generated by prayer before the proclamation of the Gospel?

An analysis of Peter's sermons, confirmed in Paul's preaching and writings, can be exceedingly profitable for us today.

For one thing, the enormity of the crucifixion was stressed: evil men killed the Son of God even as they asked life for a murderer instead. The good and righteous One was rejected in favor of a common criminal.

The vindication of Jesus Christ and his work, by the resurrection, was an ever recurring theme. Without the resurrection there would have been no preaching, no salvation, no hope, and no Church.

In early preaching, mercy and warning were combined. The Jews had crucified the Lord of Glory in ignorance, but they were now no longer ignorant. The truth eliminated any vestige of excuse and brought responsibility. To hear the Gospel was and is a great privilege, but it always carries with it a terrible responsibility.

Repentance was also a main theme of their preaching. The knowledge of the guilt of sin demanded repentance for that sin. Not only was one's mind to be changed; there also had to be a change in life itself.

This repentance invariably had certain consequences. The sins of the past were wiped out, much as one might wipe away writing on papyrus. And with remission of sins the entire future was affected. Instead of despair, there was hope; instead of weakness and futility, God-given power to overcome; instead of endless striving, rest and peace.

It is noteworthy that these early preachers believed in the sure return of Christ. The promise of Acts 1:8 would certainly be fulfilled. They knew history was going somewhere, moving with a sure tread. They knew that the God of time and eternity would ring down the curtain of history when he so willed.

These early preachers of the Word believed unswervingly that all that had happened to Christ had been foretold by the prophets. Instructed by the Lord himself, they now knew that the teachings of Moses, the prophets, and the psalms pointed primarily to Jesus Christ.

How much preaching on sin and repentance do we hear today? How really smart is a "sophistication" that denies or evades the reality of sin, with its sure judgment, and substitutes a different "gospel"?

I am convinced that if the chaos that exists in modern theological education existed instead in medical education, the health of the world would be imperiled.

Modern physicians are being trained in the basic sciences and taught how to make use of the latest advances in every field of medicine and surgery.

Modern preachers (with many wonderful exceptions) are being trained away from the simplicity of the Gospel, while the "basic science" of their calling—a heart and head knowledge of the Bible—is woefully neglected. Tragically, many come to regard Scripture as a "bent sword" and turn from it to fields of secondary importance, such as restructuring the social order. Meanwhile the souls of men continue their death march to a Christless eternity.

Many rightly are critical of a cult that denies the reality of sickness and pain. But may modern preachers evade the reality of sin and judgment to come. Concern for the ills of society should be so real that the one solution—the redemption of the individual—should be paramount. Washing the outside of the cup, or making the Prodigal comfortable, happy, and prosperous in the Far Country, is a poor substitute for preaching the new birth.

This is being written in love because of the high esteem in which I hold the Christian ministry. But if a physician is held responsible for malpractice by his fellow physicians, why should a lesser standard prevail for ministers—to whom the eternal destiny of souls is committed?

No one would wish to return to the type of medicine practiced in Luke's time. But we do need to recapture the content and relevance of the preaching of the early disciples.

*Today there is a vast difference
in the effects of . . .*

DISCIPLINE VS. PERMISSIVENESS

Recently I was the guest in a home where there are three children, ranging in age from six to eleven. These children are blessed with parents who devote a great deal of time to them, who are interested in all their friends and their school activities, and who take every possible occasion for short trips together, picnics, and other little things in which children delight. These children are secure, know they are loved, and are as happy as any I have ever seen.

But these devoted parents have also demanded and received obedience from their children. There is never any argument when they tell a child to do something, only the expectation that the command will be obeyed without question. Corporal punishment, though rare, is applied without hesitation if necessary. The parents recognize the truth found in the Book of Proverbs: "Folly is bound up in the heart of a child, but the rod of discipline drives it far from him" (22:15).

America is suffering from a generation of permissive parents who, by not requiring obedience from children, have produced teen-agers and young adults with little respect for

34

either God or man. These undisciplined young people are proving themselves a disruptive force on many school campuses, and they are a source of embarrassment and great concern to the nation. Although they are only a small minority, they are jeopardizing the entire structure of society.

Unfortunately, permissiveness is not confined to the home; it has also infected the attitudes of college and university administrations. There also have been instances where those with the authority and power to control lawlessness have failed, even watching while burning and looting were taking place. This attitude is being changed, but not before damage to the image of constituted authority has been done. Where stern measures have been taken one hears cries of "police brutality," as though those who act like hoodlums or criminals have the right to be pampered.

This attitude of permissiveness, found in homes and later transferred to our schools, has done untold harm to its victims —the young people.

In past generations the Christian home was the bulwark of the nation. The children were cherished, trained, and required to be obedient to parental authority. Have we drifted so far the other way that the future is hopeless? No, not if we are prepared to take a firm stand in training our children as they should be trained, rather than leaving them to their own devices.

In bringing up children according to God's precepts there is no room for harshness; the Bible clearly warns against this attitude. After Paul had admonished children in Ephesians 6 ("Children, obey your parents in the Lord, for this is right. 'Honor your father and mother . . . that it may be well with you and that you may live long on the earth'"), he immediately speaks to parents: "And now a word to you parents. Don't keep on scolding and nagging your children, making them angry and resentful. But bring them up with

35

the loving discipline the Lord himself approves, with suggestions and godly advice" (v. 4, "Living Letters" translation).

How can parents determine how to train their children rightly? Children can be brought up "in the discipline and instruction of the Lord" only when parents recognize the Bible as the ultimate source of reference for life. And coupled with obedient faith in God's clearly revealed truth parents must have a yearning love that softens discipline and illumines instruction, a love that the child can sense. This love is a gracious gift of the Holy Spirit.

Let no one say that the Ten Commandments are "no longer relevant" for child-rearing today. In them one finds God's moral law, which speaks precisely to us and the problems we face in a world that grows steadily more pagan. Nor is there any irrelevance in the great Bible stories, which children need to know and ponder. The story of David and Goliath, for instance, carries a compelling message of faith in God.

Give the Bible its rightful place in your home. It is from Scripture that children will learn about good and evil, right and wrong, God and Satan, Christ and redemption, heaven and hell. There they will find moral and spiritual standards on which to base convictions that will last them through life.

The Bible is plain in its teaching about morality and immorality, about purity and impurity, about honesty and dishonesty. When biblical standards are given their rightful place in the training of children as well as in the behavior of parents, one may be sure that the foundation for a Christian home has been laid.

The permissive parent and his opposite, the harsh parent, can look forward to a day when their families will rise up to smite them. Some time ago a young woman was murdered in sordid surroundings of her own choosing. Confronted with the tragedy, the grieving parents said in bewilderment, "We gave her everything she wanted"—not realizing that this itself might have been part of the cause of their sorrow.

Obviously there can be no Christian home without faith in God and in his Son. In this faith there must be evident a priority. God must come first in everything.

And because God comes first, prayer must be given its rightful place—unceasing, importunate prayer for the children and parents alike. Prayer is necessary for guidance in decision-making, not only for the seemingly "big" problems but also for the routine tasks out of which many lifelong practices and opinions proceed.

A home of stern discipline and required obedience should be a place of obvious love—love for God, of parents for each other, of parents for children, and of children for parents.

Children are amazingly astute. They can sense what parents want for them above all else. They also know whether parents are requiring of them moral and spiritual standards that they themselves do not practice. How greatly parents need the presence of the living Christ in their own lives! The greatest heritage any child can receive is the privilege of being raised in a godly home where Christ is supreme.

In a day when permissiveness has spread from careless homes into the life of our nation, even infesting the area of judicial procedures, it is the duty of every Christian to pray for a reversal of the trend. At the same time he should be setting an example for right living that can carry weight far beyond the confines of his home.

Permissiveness and disobedience breed unhappiness for all concerned, perhaps more for children and young people than we dream. Many disobedient and lawless acts are actually pleas for strict discipline.

Parental authority is a responsibility ordained by God, one for which he will give the necessary wisdom and strength. In its right exercise there is blessing for all concerned.

On the other hand, permissiveness breeds lawlessness, with tragic results for all concerned.

The wise will take heed to these words from the fifteenth chapter of First Samuel:

"Behold, to obey is better than sacrifice,
and to hearken than the fat of rams.
For rebellion is as the sin of divination,
and stubbornness is as iniquity and idolatry."

Men need confidence, but . . .

CONFIDENCE—IN WHAT?

Even a casual evaluation of the world scene today can lead to utter pessimism. But the Christian has no right to be a pessimist. He knows God and his Son. He knows, as a child of God, that nothing can happen that is outside God's will for his life.

Between the black despair of those who see a world rushing to certain judgment and the sublime confidence of some Christians, there is a great area of outlook shared by true but uninstructed Christians and others whose faith and aspirations rise no higher than man and his ability to cope with life.

Perhaps there has never been a time when so many have lacked assurance as now. Some respond by plodding through life like dumb animals. Others frantically attempt to solve problems at the human level—through committees, plans, organizations, buzzing activity. Still others give way to despair, which may lead to depression and even serious breakdown.

Why the different reactions? Why are some optimistic and others pessimistic? Can both attitudes be justified?

Perhaps the key is found in the object of confidence. If one's confidence is only in the potential and attainments of man, in nations and their power, in organizations and their human wisdom, then one has every reason to be a thorough-going pessimist. If, on the other hand, his confidence is in God—his love, goodness, power, and sovereignty—then he should be an incurable optimist.

Misplaced trust can bring disaster, but trust in God is never misplaced. It brings peace in the midst of turmoil, hope when things are at their darkest, and certainty that he never makes a mistake, that "in everything God works for good with those who love him, who are called according to his purpose" (Rom. 8:28, RSV).

Perhaps the basic cause of mental, moral, and spiritual breakdowns is uncertainty, an uncertainty that runs all through the social, economic, political, and religious thinking of many. Longing for a firm anchor and failing to find it, men feel hopelessly adrift on the sea of life.

In a time when so many are unsure of themselves, this world, and the future, the Christian has a golden opportunity to bring hope and joy to others through his confidence on Jesus Christ, the crucified and risen Son of God, who is Saviour and Lord of all who will invite him into their hearts.

There is no other foundation but Christ, no hope, peace, or certainty apart from him and his work for and in us. The words of restful assurance found in Henry F. Lyte's hymn still speak to our souls today:

> Change and decay
> In all around I see;
> O Thou who changest not,
> Abide with me.

When people have no firm foundation, they are easily shaken. Pressed by the adverse circumstances of life they will crumble like a house built upon the sand.

Three times in Psalms 42 and 43 we find the observation of a discouraged yet confident believer: "Why are you cast down, O my soul, and why are you disquieted within me? Hope in God; for I shall again praise him, my help and my God."

Has God changed? Is he not worthy of our complete confidence? Can we not look above and beyond the immediate discouragements and with the eye of faith see One who never changes and who is altogether faithful?

Why is lack of certainty so prevalent today? Why do so many drift to and fro in the tides of doubt?

The primary reason is that men do not know God or his Word. They have never experienced the saving and keeping power of Jesus Christ. And, sad to say, many through their contact with the Church have had their faith impaired and their doubts deepened.

Recently, I saw a letter from a man who had just read the revealing and alarming results of a questionnaire submitted to delegates and others attending the National Council of Churches' triennial assembly, held last December. He wrote: "As an international airline captain for twenty-five years, I wonder what kind of accident statistics we would have, and how good business would be, if 66 per cent of the captains would say on the PA system, 'Relax and enjoy the flight, ladies and gentlemen, we'll probably make it. Two-thirds of your crew believe we will get there safely.'"

He was referring to the depressing fact that to this NCC questionnaire 33 per cent of the delegates replied that they had doubts about the existence of God, 36 per cent had doubts about the deity of Christ, 31 per cent doubted whether there is life beyond the grave and 62 per cent doubted that miracles happened as recorded.

A basic reason for much uncertainty today is that in too many pulpits the trumpet gives an uncertain sound. The words of Jeremiah 2:11–13 are again being fulfilled: "Has a nation changed its gods, even though they are no gods? But my people have changed their glory for that which does not profit. Be appalled, O heavens, at this, be shocked, be utterly desolate, says the LORD, for my people have committed two evils: they have forsaken me, the fountain of living waters, and hewed out cisterns for themselves, broken cisterns, that can hold no water."

This is not an attack on the highest of all callings, that of a minister of the Gospel. It is an honest confrontation with those ministers who no longer have, or never have had, a Gospel to preach and who offer the hungry, not the Bread of Life, but the ashes of doubt.

Translate the perfidy of these false apostles into the secular realm and they would soon be denounced for the charlatans they are. Put them in the pilot's seat of a modern jet with similar doubts and uncertainties about flight plans and operational techniques, and disaster would follow. Translate the floundering opinions of some who now hold places of leadership within the Church into the practice of medicine and surgery, and death, not life, would be the lot of those patients so unfortunate as to come under their care.

God offers assurance, faith, and hope in the person of his Son and in the revelation of his truth as found in the Holy Scriptures. Here one finds the cure for pessimism in the certainty of God's loving faithfulness. In this and this alone there is serenity and peace—now and for all eternity.

There is a never-ending choice . . .

BABEL OR PENTECOST?

In seeking to be "relevant" to and "involved" with a confused generation, the Church is in danger of joining the forces of Babel. In that day men said, "Come, let us make . . . ," "Come, let us build . . . ," "Let us make a name for ourselves, lest we be scattered abroad upon the face of the whole earth" (Gen. 11:3, 4).

Feeling insecure, fearful of another flood, confident that they had within themselves the solution to their problems, the men of Babel started to make a "brave new world." What was the result? Confusion!

God had given the people of that time a revelation of his love, power, and provision. He had promised that the world would never again be destroyed by a flood. But these men rejected his love, discounted his power, ignored his provision, and disbelieved his promise. And, as always, God had the last word. He brought their plans to nought, confused their tongues, and scattered them over the face of all the earth.

There is grave danger that the Church of our day may be accepting the philosophy of Babel. By failing to fulfill its God-given mission, it is adding to the confusion of the world.

How different was Babel from Pentecost! At Pentecost, a small group of ordinary men, united in faith, hope, and prayer and obedient to the Lord's command to "wait for the promise of the Father," were suddenly transformed into flaming evangels, filled with the Holy Spirit, bearing a burning message—God's message—of redemption for a sinning world.

This event, which some saw as a confusion of tongues and others as an alcoholic binge, was actually God's empowering of man to preach the Gospel in a needy but hostile world. These men went out, not to reform the world, but to lead individual souls to redemption through faith in Jesus Christ. There was no compromise in their preaching; they knew men were lost sinners who needed to repent and believe in Christ for salvation. At the center of their message was Christ, the incarnate Son of God, who died on the Cross for sinners. This Christ arose from the dead, and the disciples bore witness to his resurrection as something of which they were certain, because they had been with him after it happened.

They showed how the truths to which they bore witness, the Christ whom they preached, were a fulfillment of Old Testament prophecy, and they repeatedly testified to the accuracy and authority of the Scriptures.

These early witnesses preached that men needed to be saved from their sins. They called for repentance and offered forgiveness in the name of their risen Lord. Their preaching was filled with deep conviction because of their own experience with Jesus Christ. They called men to make a decision, and on one occasion three thousand souls responded. At other times only a few believed, always those ordained of God unto salvation.

Their offer was universal: "And it shall be that whoever calls on the name of the Lord shall be saved" (Acts 2:21). It was the offer of an exclusive Christ: "There is salvation in no one else." It was a Gospel that divided men: some believed it, others rejected it.

These men were fully aware of the wickedness, the injustice, the evils of the social order in which they lived. They knew about the slavery, prostitution, oppression, dishonesty, and other signs of the depravity of man. And they did something about it! They knew that society would never be changed until men's hearts were changed. They knew they had the only message that could bring about that change, the message of the new birth through faith in the Risen Lord. And they gave their hearts and even their lives to the proclamation of this supernatural message of a supernatural Christ who would change men in a supernatural way.

This was the result of Pentecost. Is the organized church today following the same road? Or is it following the course of Babel?

In our world, all the basest passions of mankind seem to be coming to the fore in an orgy of lewdness, lawlessness, and strife. Many are saying that our society is "sick." But it is folly to emphasize the "corporate sins of society" without recognizing that it is the sins of *individuals* that find expression in society. From the desperately wicked hearts of men come "evil thoughts, murder, adultery, fornication, theft, false witness, slander" (Matt. 15:19). These are the things that defile a man, and they are the things that defile a society.

But what is the organized church doing about this desperate situation? Is it playing the part of the medical quack who offers various nostrums and panaceas, or the medical hack who tries to relieve symptoms without concern for the underlying disease, instead of offering a clear diagnosis and cure based on God's word? Is it slighting Pentecost, with all its attendant power and blessing, in favor of Babel, with its confusion, frustration, and defeat?

I am greatly concerned about the Church. I am heartsick over a widespread shift in emphasis, a shift from proclamation of the Gospel of Jesus Christ as the one cure for sin, to "involvement" in any and every activity designed for social change, with seemingly little concern for the basic change of heart that is the product of the Gospel.

Has the Church lost faith in the power of the Gospel? Does it think it can redeem society without touching the hearts of individuals? Does it think it can join forces with the world to build a city and make a name while it ignores the biblical truth that believers are strangers and exiles on the earth, looking to "the city which has foundations, whose builder and maker is God" (Heb. 11:10)?

A study of the convocations of most of the major denominations reveals that their main concerns are becoming secular and materialistic rather than spiritual. The Gospel is at best taken for granted and not emphasized, and at worst denied.

Can the situation be reversed? The answer is an emphatic *yes*. But to do so we must turn away from Babel, with its call to merely human achievement, and turn back to Pentecost, where the power of the God of eternity was manifested in the presence and person of his Spirit. This will happen when men bow their minds, wills, and hearts to him in humble faith and obedience. If they do this, the Church will be revived and will go out into this sinning, lost world with the one and only message that will work—that "Christ died for our sins in accordance with the scriptures, that he was buried, that he was raised on the third day in accordance with the scriptures" (I Cor. 15:3, 4). This message, the Apostle Paul says, is of "first importance"!

Babel or Pentecost—which will the Church choose?

As we read the daily newspapers
and news magazines
we are forced to ask . . .

WHAT'S WRONG?

What's wrong with the world? It may well be likened to a ship at sea, without captain, compass, helm, or chart, with all radio contact lost, and at the mercy of a mutinous crew. Our world is in desperate straits and headed for disaster.

And it is all so needless! God has given his Son to be Captain and his Spirit as the helm to guide through the perils of life. He has given the Holy Scriptures as man's chart and compass. And he has even set up a two-way means of communication with himself—prayer.

To reject the authority of the Holy Scriptures is to be tossed hither and yon by the conflicting opinions of men. To reject Jesus Christ as Saviour of the soul and Lord of life is to choose the course of folly. To refuse the guidance of the Holy Spirit is to go on in darkness. To neglect prayer is to lose the channel to and from God's infinite love and wisdom.

It would be the height of folly to try to steer a ship without the necessary means of navigation; and with a mutinous crew aboard, nothing less than disaster could be expected. How then can we look for anything better for a

47

world that is run by men who ignore the Captain and Owner and trust in their own wisdom even while they live in rebellion?

What's wrong with the world?

Is it not drifting helplessly toward the rocks of destruction because it is no longer anchored in God's holy truth, the only foundation for time and for eternity? Is it not blind to the solution of its problems because it has rejected God's answer and his way in favor of its own?

The wisdom of this world inevitably produces a faulty compass and man-made chart. It offers "guidance" that steers in the wrong direction. It communicates with men but not with God. And it readily accepts the leadership of Satan, the ancient enemy of souls. Most deplorable of all, perhaps, is the fact that one hears in the cacophony of voices those of other mutineers—false prophets who should be leaders but who now deny the authority of the Captain and the accuracy of his chart and compass.

And so, like dumb animals being led to slaughter, men and nations rush on in their folly until judgment falls. Like a ship helpless in the storm, they are caught in the waves of judgment, to perish on the rocks of futility.

"Crisis," "revolution," "change"—these are the words of today. No one would deny that the world is in crisis. There are seemingly insoluble problems. There is a cry for revolution and change. But the crisis is not found at the point where men place it, nor can it be met by the revolutionary changes many advocate.

Man fails to see that the "crisis" stems from his rejection or ignoring of God. Revolution and change is needed in the *hearts* of men, not primarily in their environment. The solution of the world's problems is far removed from any organization. It rests in the person and work of Jesus Christ, the Son of God.

But the mutinous crew of earthbound strategists reject God's solution in favor of something they hope to concoct. Philosophers rise no higher than the acme of human wisdom and understanding. Scientists discover no more than what God has created. False prophets deny the verities of the faith while they deify man and humanize God. Little wonder that the rebellion grows, even as danger looms nearer.

Men and nations need to heed God's warning:

"What fools the nations are to rage against the Lord! How strange that men should try to outwit God!

"For a summit conference of the nations has been called to plot against the Lord and His Messiah, Christ the King.

"'Come, let us break His chains,' they say, 'and free ourselves from all this slavery to God.'

"But God in heaven merely laughs! He is amused by all their puny plans.

"And then in fierce fury He rebukes them and fills them with fear.

"For the Lord declares, 'This is the King of My choice, and I have enthroned Him in Jerusalem, My holy city.'

"His chosen One replies, 'I will reveal the everlasting purposes of God, for the Lord has said to Me, "You are My Son. This is Your Coronation Day. Today I am giving You Your glory."'

"'Only ask and I will give You all the nations of the world.

"'Rule them with a rod of iron; smash them like pots!'"

"O kings and rulers of the earth, listen while there is time.

"Serve the Lord with reverent fear; rejoice with trembling.

"Fall down before His Son and kiss His feet before His anger is roused and you perish. I am warning you—His wrath will soon begin. But, oh, the joys of those who put their trust in Him!" (Psalm 2, from *Living Psalms*, paraphrased by Kenneth Taylor; copyright Tyndale House Foundation, 1967; used by permission).

What's wrong with the world?

Nothing that cannot be solved by God's love and grace! Why, then, is man determined to go his way and solve his own problems without reference to God, thus making shipwreck of his world?

If there is nothing wrong with men and nations for which God has not made full provision, the difficulty, then, obviously lies with man's own pride, unbelief, and disobedience, which have culminated in a situation in many ways analogous to that of the ship described above.

And this is where the Church comes into the picture. To the Church has been entrusted the Gospel of redemption. It exists to witness to its Lord. Its chart and compass are the Holy Scriptures. Its contact is with the throne of grace, and its message is directed to the mutineers.

God forbid that the church should fail to evaluate the situation rightly; that it should bypass the message of salvation in favor of social action or anything else; that it should sin against the Lord by playing down his person and work; that it should find fault with the Bible, its sole chart and compass; that it should overlook the duty and privilege of prayer; and, worst of all, that it should join itself with the mutineers!

The siren call for revolution and reformation is heard on every hand. This appeals to man's pride of accomplishment.

But the call of God is for men to be reconciled to him through the blood of his Son shed on the Cross of Calvary.

Man continues today as always to find this an "offense" because of its demand for humility, faith, and obedience.

We know of the danger of continued refusal to heed God's call.

How do we respond?

The fact is, Christianity is both . . .

SUPERNATURAL AND MIRACULOUS

Every Evangelical finds himself confronted with the danger of slipping into the ever-hardening attitude of the Pharisee while every theological liberal is confronted with the dangers inherent in the "doctrine" of the Sadducees. These dangers, present in all generations, are perhaps greater today than ever before, as the lines between "conservatives" and "modernists" are being drawn more clearly.

Of the Pharisees our Lord said, "In vain do they worship me, teaching as doctrines the precepts of men" (Matt. 15:9), while to the Sadducees, questioning him about the resurrection of the dead, his reply was, "You are wrong, because you know neither the scriptures nor the power of God" (Matt. 22:29).

Evangelicals need very much to be warned of the dangers of pharisaism, with its legalism and its negative approach to the Christian faith, and I will write on this another time. For now I am thinking of the growing evidence that many in the major denominations who hold positions of great power are not far removed from the Sadducees of our Lord's time.

The chief characteristic of the Sadducees was a type of

religious rationalism that denied the realm of the supernatural with its angels and spirits and wholly rejected the doctrine of the resurrection. As has been said by such men as Machen, "Eliminate the supernatural and the miraculous and there is no such thing as Christianity." How we need to stress this today.

Without the supernatural there is no such thing as the virgin birth, the miracles, the atonement, the resurrection, or prayer. Indeed, eliminate the supernatural and there can be no God, no incarnation of God in the person of His Son, the Lord Jesus Christ, and, of course, no Holy Spirit.

In other words, the minute one begins to tamper with God's supernatural being and his manifestations in supernatural and miraculous ways, he is tampering with the foundational realities of the Christian faith.

The advances made by science stagger the imagination. The Apollo 8 triumph, for instance, has added another dimension to the marvels of modern scientific achievement. But never let us presume to conform God to the limitations of human achievement, for man discovers only what God has created and the laws of the universe that are a part of that creation.

The growing tendency to eliminate the supernatural, or the miraculous, in connection with the Christian faith is one that cannot be countenanced by those who hold to the nature and validity of that faith. Our faith is based, not on man-made dogmas and opinions, but on a divine revelation, supernatural in its nature and miraculous in its effect.

Wherever the natural is substituted for the supernatural or the miraculous nature of the work of the Holy Spirit held in question, effective Christian witness dies. Tragically, we see death in many areas of the Church, because there are those who limit God by their own limitations while they talk and work in terms compatible with those of the secularists and materialists.

The current pressure to secularize the Church is the result of a confusion over both its nature and its message. The need is not to make the Church popular with the world but to show the power of the Holy Spirit to transform lives, and the miracles that take place in the life of one who has had this experience with the living Christ.

Believing neither in the actuality of the Holy Spirit as a Person nor in the supernatural effect he has in the lives of those who have gone through the supernatural experience of being "born again" (a biblical term that is very unwelcome among many modern Sadducees), some are projecting an image of the Church that is tied to man rather than to God, and to secular activities without reference to this miraculous change.

The modern Sadducee considers himself a realist, in tune with the world and committed to the discoveries and advances of science. The Christian is indeed a realist, but he knows that his faith is based in a supernatural person and that this destiny has no reference to, nor can it be affected by, *anything* man can do.

I have recently studied intensively the records of the early Church as found in the Acts of the Apostles and in the Epistles of Paul, James, Peter, and John. The Church began in unlikely soil and was confronted by overwhelming obstacles, but not once did the Apostles seek to identify it with the existing social order. It was a supernatural organism existing in a naturalistic world. Its members expected and experienced multiplied evidences of the miraculous character of their faith—faith that changed men and revolutionized the social order, not by secular activism but by the work of the Holy Spirit.

The Church and individual Christians lose their effectiveness as they go the way of the secularist. They also lose the warmth and the light that characterize persons and groups who have had an encounter with Christ.

As was true in our Lord's day, so today the Church is suffering from those who "know neither the scriptures nor the power of God." To a tragic number of "Christians" the Bible is a closed book. Regarding it as no longer relevant to this scientific age, they close their minds to its supernatural message and the miraculous effect it has on those who take it as spiritual food and divine wisdom. Furthermore, never having experienced the power of God in their own lives, they ignore its availability for themselves and for those to whom they minister.

Recently, at a student conference dominated by men with a new concept of the mission and message of the Church, a student complained that during two days there had not been one prayer. From the leader he received this reply: "I am sorry that you have not been praying. Everything we do is prayer—cleaning your teeth or any other activity."

What price secularization!

The Church—and individual Christians—need to rediscover that we are dealing with a supernatural God. Let him speak: "For thus says the LORD, who created the heavens (he is God!), who formed the earth and made it (he established it; he did not create it a chaos, he formed it to be inhabited!): I am the LORD, and there is no other" (Isa. 45:18).

The view of this world from the Apollo capsule was an awesome and thrilling sight to behold. Let the Sadducee stop and remember that we are dealing with the Creator of the universe, the magnitude and complexity of which staggers the mind. This should certainly bring us to our knees in worship.

54

*We can but ask what has happened
and is now happening to . . .*

THE TWO KINDS OF SEEDS?

What happened to the seed of the Gospel that was planted
in your heart? Is it bringing forth a harvest for righteousness,
or has it disappeared?

Many of our Lord's parables were left for interpretation
to those who in spiritual matters had seeing eyes and hearing
ears. But the parable of the sower (Matt. 13:1-9, 18-23) was
explained in detail, not only for the disciples but for all
who down through the ages have desired an explanation of
the world situation and of what happens when the Gospel
is preached.

In this graphic story our Lord tells of the dangers that
beset all to whom the Gospel is preached—the attacks of
Satan and the various kinds of erosion of faith—and also
of the blessings that proceed from the believing and faithful
heart.

The seed is, of course, the Gospel of God's redeeming
work in Christ, and the different kinds of ground are the
hearts and minds of men to whom the Gospel is preached.

This parable, like the rest of the Bible, teaches that there
is a vast difference in the ultimate destinies of the souls of

men, and that there is a sense in which we are directly and personally responsible for accepting or rejecting the grace of God.

Strange to say, some have interpreted this story as proof that one-fourth of those who hear the Gospel are saved. Jesus was speaking, not about percentages, but about four kinds of hearts.

The hard ground. Some who hear the Gospel are spiritually obtuse—not through ignorance, but through a willful indifference to the good news. Satan snatches away the seed, leaving the hardened, barren heart as it was before. (One wonders in passing why, when Jesus spoke so specifically about the person and work of the devil, so many deny that he exists.)

The Apostle Paul also describes the hardened heart and offers an explanation: "Even if our gospel is veiled, it is veiled only to those who are perishing. In their case the god of this world has blinded the minds of unbelievers, to keep them from seeing the light of the gospel of the glory of Christ, who is the likeness of God (II Cor. 4:3-4).

This condition is unrelated to intelligence. The unintelligent and unsophisticated can grasp spiritual truth and accept it, and the wise and prudent of this world may be spiritually blind. Thank God for the fact that the good seed cannot be snatched away from the humbled and softened heart that turns to him in simple faith!

The rocky soil. This is the heart of the person who weighs the benefits of the goodness and mercy of God against the temporary discomfort of becoming an alien in a hostile world, against the demands of the Christian life and the suffering it sometimes entails, and, after the weighing, turns back to the world. In such a person the seed is lost; something else takes its place.

The Apostle Paul, after suffering untold trials, persecutions, and personal loss, evaluated the choice in these words: "I consider that the sufferings of this present time are not worth comparing with the glory that is to be revealed to us" (Rom. 8:18).

God never promised his children freedom from trouble—only the grace to bear it. He never promised freedom from persecution; in fact, Scripture says that "all who desire to live a godly life in Christ Jesus will be persecuted" (II Tim. 3:12). But always we are assured of his grace.

Jesus, speaking of the one whose heart is like rocky soil, said, "When tribulation or persecution arises on account of the word, immediately he falls away" (Matt. 13:21b). Can you "take it" for Christ? There are tens of thousands in the world today who stand as good soldiers of Jesus Christ, suffering for his name's sake. They put you and me to shame —we who have never suffered anything but rather have ridden on the wave of a popular religion without depth.

Thorns. Ah, here we are on truly dangerous ground—more dangerous than tribulation or persecution, because the danger is so pleasant to take.

The normal pressures of everyday life can choke the seed of the Gospel into unfruitfulness if "doing" and "being" take precedence over the things that will last for eternity. Economic success, affluence, the pleasant sense of material sufficiency, the "delight in riches" of which our Lord speaks, can destroy the Gospel's effect.

To forget that man does not live by bread alone is to suffer a perilous lapse. Letting tangible things take precedence over the unseen but real blessings of God is a sure way to spiritual oblivion—and how many follow that course!

When the affairs of this world loom above those of God's Kingdom, man stands on the brink of disaster. Paul says, "We look not to the things that are seen but to the things

57

that are unseen; for the things that are seen are transient, but the things that are unseen are eternal" (II Cor. 4:18).

A man may revel in every comfort and luxury this world can afford, only to have them all vanish in the reality of God's eternity. He who says to his soul, "Soul, you have ample goods laid up for many years; take your ease—eat, drink, be merry," will one day hear God say, "Fool!"

The good soil. When the seed of the Gospel falls on good ground, a tremendous change takes place. A man hears the word, and the Holy Spirit enables him to understand it. What once seemed foolish to him becomes the most wonderful thing in the world. He hears the word as God's truth, believes, and obeys. The Bible describes the process: "Man believes with his heart and so is justified, and he confesses with his lips and so is saved" (Rom. 10:10).

That is only the beginning. The harvest is seen in a transformed life and in a consistent witness to others, so that a person's salvation, his newness in Christ, is multiplied in the lives of others who also hear and believe.

Remember who told this story and gave its interpretation: the Lord of History, the God of Glory, the Creator and Preserver of all; the One who is, who was, and who is to come!

He who is wise will beware of the dangers that surround him—the "spiritual hosts of wickedness in the heavenly places," the diversions and cares of the world, those urges and tendencies to do evil that are ever within us.

Surely we will be wise to search our own hearts and lives to see what has priority. The seed of the Gospel has been sown in our hearts; what has happened to it? The first seed described in the parable was destroyed by the devil, the second by the world, and the third by the flesh. Have the world, the flesh, and the devil had their way in our hearts and destroyed what should have changed our lives for now and for eternity?

The Holy Spirit gives life. It is he who takes the seed of the Gospel and brings forth an abundant harvest in the lives of those who believe and obey.

Time is running out, this is a matter of . . .

URGENCY

Has the church lost its sense of urgency in evangelism? Has it substituted something irrelevant for God's provision for crisis? Has it misunderstood the nature of the world's predicament?

The Apostle Paul, writing to his spiritual son, Timothy, says: "Preach the word, be urgent in season and out of season, convince, rebuke, and exhort, be unfailing in patience and in teaching" (II Tim. 4:2). Phillips arrests our attention with this translation, "Never lose your sense of urgency."

Paul's appeal for urgency is based on the kingship of Christ, who will judge all men on the return of Christ, which will ring down the curtain of history as we know it; and on the coming of a new kingdom, the kingdom of Christ.

The sense of urgency is heightened, Paul says, by the fact that a time is coming when men will be unwilling to listen to the gospel message: "The time is coming when people will not endure sound teaching, but having itching ears they will accumulate for themselves teachers to suit their own likings, and will turn away from listening to the truth and wander into myths" (II Tim. 4:3, 4).

Everywhere today we hear of a world in crisis—race, food, economics, population explosion, conflicting ideologies, all magnified by selfishness, hatred, greed, lust, and other sins of the human heart.

The Church is found at the forefront in this cry of "crisis," but it seems at times to be merely frenzied about *symptoms* while oblivious to the source and nature of the crisis.

Picture the emergency ward of a large and well-equipped modern hospital. A man is carried in on a stretcher. His face is contorted with pain, his right leg is flexed, and he places a protective hand on his abdomen.

Nurses and doctors hurry in, and a laboratory technician is called. The patient's temperature is above normal; he is nauseated; the pain, originating in the pit of his stomach, has now localized in his lower right abdomen. A stat blood count shows a marked increase in leukocytes (nature's army of defense against infection), and there is a "shift to the left" in the differential count, showing that the process of infection is advancing.

Suppose the doctors give an injection to relieve the pain, use medicines to lower the temperature, place an ice bag on his abdomen to cool the area, give a sedative to relieve the nausea and a transfusion to make the blood picture more normal. Then they place the patient in a comfortable bed and hope he will get well.

From this picture even the least informed layman has probably deduced that the patient has an acutely inflamed appendix. Does he need palliative treatment? Is the alleviation of his *symptoms* the cure for his disease? Are not those responsible for his care culpable if they either misdiagnose or mistreat his condition? And are they not made even more culpable by the fact that the facilities and means of treatment are immediately available? The answer is obvious.

We are living in a time of crisis. The symptoms are to be seen on every hand. All the mass media display for our eyes and din into our ears evidence that men and nations are passing through a series of convulsions.

But has God been taken by surprise? Is his solution for the problems of the world different from what it was in the first Christian century? Is the Gospel, powerful enough then to overcome every obstacle, no longer capable of producing change? Is the crisis so great that the Cross of Jesus Christ must be bypassed? Is it no longer true that Christ is man's only hope of redemption? Has the wisdom of man transcended the infinite knowledge of God?

Paul told Timothy to "preach the word." Nothing was said about offering homilies on "being good." Nor did he tell Timothy to work up a demonstration against the tyrannies of Rome or the degrading traffic in slaves. He did not inveigh against Greek philosophy, nor did he try to drive a wedge between the poor and the rich. His admonition was to "preach the word," and no doubt Timothy knew as well as Paul that what was "of first importance" in this preaching was "that Christ died for our sins in accordance with the scriptures, that he was buried, that he was raised on the third day in accordance with the scriptures" (I Cor. 15:3, 4).

What utter foolishness, you say? How could a message like that transform men and society?

And it was then, this message of the Cross is folly to the world, even though it is God's answer to the crisis of men and nations. And if this simple message of God's offer of redemption to sinners becomes foolishness to the visible church also, then the world will indeed be in desperate straits! Part of the crisis is precisely at that point.

Life is by no means static, and the mistakes of today can snowball into the disasters of tomorrow. Concern with symptoms is good to a point, for it shows awareness of impending danger. It is tragic, however, if the Church's response to crisis becomes simply a nebulous affirmation that "the Church is mission" (whatever that means) rather than the bold declaration that Jesus Christ came into the world and died for us sinners and that he arose again from the dead. Nor does the message stop there. It is the message of a coming King and the setting up of his eternal kingdom.

To the call for "involvement" our response is, "Of course!" But what shall the Church be involved in? Not, surely, in becoming a part of a lost world order, but rather, as a called out people, in bearing witness to Christ's love and redeeming power in a festering social order.

Crisis is all about us—in the lives of individuals, in the life of our nation, in the world as a whole. But there is no crisis for which God does not have the answer. To the Church and individual Christians he has entrusted his formula for solving the situation.

Not long ago I received a letter from a school teacher in one of the most sophisticated high schools in Texas. The children she teaches come from homes deeply involved in the space age. But the church she has attended and others of which she is aware are also sophisticated—preaching "another gospel" and frantically trying to solve the world's problems without reference to the Gospel of personal redemption. She wrote, "Much is being said about 'experimental ministries.' I would be thankful if those responsible would make it possible for us to have in this area a church where the simple Gospel of Jesus Christ is preached, and give us two years to try the 'experiment.'"

Have we lost our sense of urgency? Have we lost confidence in God's remedy? Are we now so far removed from God's methods of solving crises that we are completely insensitive to his Spirit's leading? Has the magnitude of the world's problems blinded our eyes to the *power* of the Gospel, of the Holy Spirit, and of prayer?

How wonderful if the Church could shift its emphasis from new programs and pressures for church union to a simple preaching, teaching, and living of Jesus Christ, the crucified Son of God! Our Lord is the "Christ of every crisis." Let's give him a chance.

Yes, there is . . .

DANGER AHEAD

"Danger ahead" signs on the highways . . . "Danger" on bottles that contain poison . . . "Beware of the Propellers" at some airfields . . . "Thin Ice" on ponds and rivers in the winter . . . "Cross at Intersections" . . . "Beware of the Dog" . . . "Speed Limit . . ."—all of us live with warnings on every hand. We take them as a matter of course, and if we stop to think we are thankful for them. We know they are meant for our good.

Strange to say, however, many of us resent any word of warning about our spiritual welfare. The possibility of danger in regard to our eternal destiny is only too often hidden by a conspiracy of silence. Now that the reality of the devil and of hell are ridiculed, even by many who teach and preach, it has become passé to speak of sin and judgment and the world to come.

Men in many secular fields recognize their responsibility to warn of particular dangers. State and federal laws require that there be clear and adequate warnings against certain hazards. But many ministers of the Gospel are silent about the Bible's warning of "the wrath to come"—a subject about

65

which Jesus, John the Baptist, Matthew, Luke, and John speak clearly.

John, in the Revelation, describes a day when the wrath of the spurned Christ will be poured out: "Then the kings of the earth and the great men and the generals and the rich and the strong, and every one, slave and free, hid in the caves and among the rocks of the mountains, calling to the mountains and rocks, 'Fall on us and hide us from the face of him who is seated on the throne, and from the wrath of the Lamb; for the great day of their wrath has come, and who can stand before it?'" (6:15–17, RSV).

Why is there silence on this subject about which God so clearly warns us in the Bible?

Why do men ignore the whole matter of a coming judgment, mentioned more than 1,000 times in Scripture?

Why do many of those who should proclaim the truth of wrath, judgment, and future punishment remain mute, or soothe with platitudes that please even as they damn?

The reason is not hard to find. They preach a deformed doctrine of God, a doctrine in which his love and mercy are stressed while his holiness, justice, and judgment are slighted.

Certainly the Bible comforts us with the truth that "God is love"; yet it also warns us that "our God is a consuming fire." The Bible that tells us that Christ is a foundation stone, a sure footing, the only foundation, also warns that "every one who falls on that stone will be broken to pieces; but when it falls on any one it will crush him" (Luke 20:18).

By and large churchgoers hear messages of comfort and hope based on wishful thinking. The nature of sin, an offense against a holy God, is denied or disregarded. The Cross is spoken of solely in terms of love without the element of propitiation. Only the physical agony of Christ on the cross is stressed; his role as sin-bearer and his vicarious death are overlooked.

I do not see how God can fail to judge those who preach or teach a gospel that is not *the* Gospel. The love, death, and resurrection of Jesus Christ must be preached against the backdrop of the holiness and judgment of God, who offered his Son as a substitute and as the One to whom we may turn for salvation.

No nation has ever existed under more favorable circumstances than America. None has had greater privileges and opportunities. Yet like Israel of old, we have turned every man to his own way. And where there is no repentance, God's judgment is there.

Where are those who should stand in the highways and byways to warn this sinning nation? We are being warned about man's offenses against man, his inhumanity to his fellows—and we need this warning. But how few speak also of our offenses against a holy God! How few preach of things beyond the grave. How many stand up to preach about "justice" but fail to mention "self-control and future judgment" (Acts 24:25). How appallingly evident it is that the Church today is more concerned with man's temporary material welfare than with the welfare of his eternal soul.

The Apostle Paul, preaching to the intellectuals in Athens, told them of God as Creator and Sustainer of life and of man's vain attempts to worship him by man-made contrivances. Then he said, "The times of ignorance God overlooked, but now he commands all men everywhere to repent, because he has fixed a day on which he will judge the world in righteousness by a man whom he has appointed, and of this he has given assurance to all men by raising him from the dead" (Acts 17:30, 31).

Why so few sermons on "repentance"? Or on that coming "day"? Or on the certainty of coming judgment?

The only explanation is that many no longer admit or believe in the true nature of sin, so deadly in its effect that only the atoning sacrifice of the Son of God can save its victims. And because the biblical teaching about sin is rejected, the biblical teaching about judgment and redemption is rejected also.

The good news is what God has done at Calvary and continues to do for man. But salvation is not offered on man's terms. It is offered on God's terms, and it involves sin and judgment, love and redemption. No part is complete without the others. Too often a truncated gospel is preached that either denies or ignores the "day" about which our Lord warned, a day of finality and judgment toward which all are headed but from which all may escape by way of the Cross of Christ.

God's infinite patience is seen by many today as indifference rather than forbearance, blindness rather than loving hope. The Apostle Peter tells us that God does not wish that "any should perish, but that all should reach repentance. But the day of the Lord will come like a thief, and then the heavens will pass away with a loud noise, and the elements will be dissolved with fire, and the earth and the works that are upon it will be burned up" (II Pet. 3:9, 10).

Figurative language? Don't rest on a false hope! And why rest at all on anything less than Jesus and his atoning, forgiving, cleansing work?

But, you say, this introduces the element of fear, and fear is incompatible with our thoughts of a God of love. For the unrepentant sinner there *is* danger, and he *should* fear. The future is incredibly dark for the unbeliever. It is the part of honesty and love to warn where danger exists.

Paul says, "Therefore, knowing the fear of the Lord, we persuade men" (II Cor. 5:11a). And to Timothy he said, "Never lose your sense of urgency, in season or out of season" (II Tim. 4:2a, Phillips).

There is danger ahead for the unbeliever. And there is perfect safety for all who believe.

*There's a vast and eternal
difference between the . . .*

SPIRITUAL VS. SECULAR

"What is the difference between spiritual and secular, if any?"

This question recently came to me from a minister to students in one of our state universities. From information from a number of other sources, I have come to realize that the blurring of the distinction between things spiritual and things secular is widespread among activistic ministers, men who seemingly feel that their primary calling is to bring about social change.

No one can exist without engaging in secular activities, and there is nothing inherently evil either in secular pursuits or in many of the material things that are a part of our life on this earth. But if we fail to understand the importance of the spiritual as compared with the secular, we can in that failure lose the meaning and values of Christianity.

The difference between secular and spiritual is the difference between time and eternity, between body and soul, between earth and heaven, between sight and faith. Our Lord brings this difference into clear perspective when he

70

asks, "What is a man profited, if he shall gain the whole world, and lose his own soul?" (Matt. 16:26a).

The Apostle Paul states the difference in words no one should misunderstand: "We look not at the things which are seen, but at the things which are not seen: for the things which are seen are temporal; but the things which are not seen are eternal" (II Cor. 4:18).

Probably all of us have heard the cliché about the person who is "so heavenly minded that he is of no earthly use," and there may be some people to whom it applies. But the statements and activities of many today show them to be so earthly minded that they fail to realize that after death there is an eternity to be spent, either in God's presence or separated from him. God entered human history in the person of his Son not only to proclaim the concept of eternal life for man but also to provide the way whereby the transition from spiritual death to spiritual life could take place.

The welfare of the body is largely a matter of secular and material advantages. The welfare of the soul is a matter of man's relationship with God through the Lord Jesus Christ.

It is only through the Holy Spirit that man comes to a knowledge of and surrender to God. Unless the Spirit draws him, he does not come to God. Unless the Spirit instructs and enlightens him, he remains in ignorance. "The natural man receiveth not the things of the Spirit of God: for they are foolishness unto him: neither can he know them, because they are spiritually discerned" (I Cor. 2:14).

The distance between secular and spiritual is so vast that only God could span it. And this he has done. The secular is the realm of the body and its surroundings; the spiritual reaches beyond the horizon of this earth and on into the boundless vista of eternity.

The secular is apprehended by the senses, the spiritual

by faith. The secular ends with death; the spiritual enters into its greatest glory after death.

The dominion of the secular is only temporary. The triumph of the spiritual brings an eternal weight of glory.

The primary concern of the secular is material welfare and comforts. The primary concern of the spiritual is redemption and obedience to God's revealed will. And the Christian's primary desire is that all men shall hear the message of redemption.

There is constant tension between the secular and the spiritual for they are of two worlds. Christ makes this very plain: "If ye were of the world, the world would love his own: but because ye are not of the world . . . therefore the world hateth you" (John 15:19).

What a man wears and eats and the condition of his external surroundings are all part of his secular existence. What a man is inside determines his spiritual state, and this needs transformation by the Spirit of God.

The Gospel is the message of God's offer to transform a person from a secular man into a spiritual one. This means, not that he will no longer be concerned about secular affairs, but that he will regard them in the perspective of eternity.

The aged Apostle John makes the distinction very clear: "Love not the world, neither the things that are in the world. If any man love the world, the love of the Father is not in him. For all that is in the world, the lust of the flesh, and the lust of the eyes, and the pride of life, is not of the Father, but is of the world. And the world passeth away, and the lust thereof: but he that doeth the will of God abideth for ever" (I John 2:15-17).

The secular is man's natural condition; the spiritual is his redeemed condition. This means not that all man's natural condition is evil but that there is a state available to man that is beyond anything this world can offer.

For the secular mind, the Cross of Christ is utter foolishness. For the spiritual mind, it is the power of God unto salvation to all who accept its message.

The Christian must exercise certain secular concerns. He must have love and compassion that issues in help for those in need. Our Lord set an example when he healed the sick and fed the hungry. But the healing and the feeding were not ends in themselves, for Christ taught that man does not live by bread alone and that his highest need is met only when he becomes a new person in Christ.

To ignore human need is to deny some of our Lord's most clearly taught lessons. But to ignore man's spiritual need is to deny the reason for his coming into the world.

The Church is in the world to bear a spiritual witness to the eternal verities. If she conforms to worldly standards and values, she loses her influence. She must stand as a spiritual light in a secular setting.

The Apostle Paul voices a truth and a warning as relevant today as it was for the people of Corinth nearly twenty centuries ago: "If our gospel be hid, it is hid to them that are lost: in whom the god of this world hath blinded the minds of them which believe not, lest the light of the glorious gospel of Christ, who is the image of God, should shine unto them" (II Cor. 4:3, 4).

Secularism, as such, is a grave danger, and never has it been more so than today. Paul speaks of this danger, as seen in those "who changed the truth of God into a lie, and worshipped and served the creature more than the Creator, who is blessed for ever" (Rom. 1:25).

Primary concern with the secular not only dims a sensitivity to spiritual values but also shifts the emphasis of the Gospel away from the Cross and to things that perish with the using. On the other hand, the individual Christian and the Church that keep the secular and spiritual in their proper perspective will be "salt" and "light" in the midst of decay and darkness.

All around us there are . . .

PITFALLS

All that most people in the world see of Christ is what they see of him in the lives of Christians. If we do not honor him in our relations with others, we fail at the point that really counts.

We who identify ourselves as evangelicals are often guilty of attitudes and behavior totally inconsistent with our Christian profession. Although we strongly assert our concern for the verities of the faith, we too easily show little of the presence and power of the Holy Spirit in our lives.

It is sobering to realize that we can destroy our Christian witness by a careless word or thoughtless action. Observers may say, "If that is the meaning of being a Christian, I want no part of it."

One of the pitfalls for the theologically conservative is spiritual pride. Convinced of the facts of our faith, we may forget that it is not orthodoxy that saves but Jesus Christ. We rightly believe the biblical revelation of Christ's person and work; but we may develop pride in our faith rather than in the saving grace of God.

Another pitfall is the ever present tendency to be pharisaical, to thank God that we are not as other men. We pat ourselves on the back because we are not guilty of some weakness we see in others or do not have some habit we regard with distaste. Many true Christians are excluded from fellowship by other Christians who regard themselves too highly. Let us beware lest we sin against God and our brothers in this matter. We can reach others only where they are, not where we wish them to be. That was our Lord's approach and it must be ours. To draw about us the cloak of self-righteousness smothers our witness.

Some years ago a dedicated minister worked for months trying to lead a rather notorious character in his community to the Lord. Finally he succeeded in getting the man to agree to come to a church dinner where a businessman was to give his witness to the power of Christ. When the man arrived at the church, the odor of alcohol was strong on his breath. Aware of it and embarrassed, he said to the minister, "I think I should leave." The minister replied: "No, you stick with me and no one will know which of us smells of liquor." His sense of humor (he had never taken a drink in his life) along with his loving attitude won that man to the Lord, and in succeeding years the man became an outstanding Christian. We all must realize, as this minister did, that in seeking to win men to Christ, we must accept them as they are.

In these days when there is so much emphasis on social reform, when social betterment seems to have crowded out the Gospel of redemption from sin in the minds of some, there is a real danger that in reaction to this imbalance we will neglect our clear responsibility to the needy. Compassion and loving concern must be a part of the life of the Christian. Without them our profession is empty. With them the love of Christ can make our witness effective.

Worsening race relations in many areas bring another call

to Christians to search their own hearts. Christian race relations begin in our attitudes and continue in our outward contacts with others. We deplore violence in others; but are we ourselves always courteous and considerate, always concerned to create a climate in which the love of Christ can be manifested?

Another pitfall for the evangelical is the development of a spirit that actually rejoices in evil. Contrary to Paul's admonition, we *rejoice* in iniquity and revel in the moral and spiritual failures of others. How interesting it is to savor a juicy story about some Christian who has fallen! And how often we forget that we too might be tempted and fall.

To the discredit of those involved, Christian fellowship has sometimes been broken over secondary matters, things on which godly people often differ. This does not honor the Lord nor further the work of God's Kingdom.

Do we have a chip on our shoulder? Do we carry around a set of hypersensitive feelings? Do we go about looking for defects in others? Such attitudes make the bearer miserable, as well as those who must deal with him.

Many conservatives fail inexcusably in the matter of common courtesy and graciousness. I know some extreme liberals who put us to shame by their kindness and consideration of others. Paul's word to Timothy speaks to all Christians: "The Lord's servant must not be quarrelsome but kindly to every one . . ." (II Tim. 2:24, RSV). How often we forget that "a soft answer turneth away wrath,"—with disastrous results to our effective Christian witness!

Some persons who are widely reputed to be conservative Christians lead lives totally inconsistent with their professions. Some engage in immorality or other disgraceful behavior even as they proclaim their orthodoxy. Did you say,

"Impossible for me"? "Let any one who thinks that he stands take heed lest he fall" (I Cor. 10:12).

Boasting of one's orthodoxy is a pitfall into which some fall. Our boast is in nothing we are or do but only in the redeeming grace of a loving God. Spurious spirituality is easily recognized. A trust in orthodoxy as an end in itself is presumption at best and often pure pharisaism.

For any Christian, the lack of an adequate devotional life means spiritual starvation. I have known people who affirmed their faith in the Bible "from cover to cover" but who at the same time knew nothing about it. Their affirmation may have sounded pious, but their ignorance of the Word revealed the true state of their hearts. Likewise, without a prayer life in which prayer is as natural as breathing, the spiritual nature shrivels and dies.

Then, too, there is a form of spiritual laziness that presumes on the grace of God and stunts spiritual growth. Orthodoxy is no excuse for laziness. Christ has saved us to serve him and our fellow man. We cannot hide behind a façade of conservative beliefs while we do nothing to witness to the love of God.

The Christian who honors his Lord is not the one who, like the Pharisees, boasts of his orthodoxy but the one who day by day seizes every opportunity God gives him and tries in every way possible to glorify the One who has redeemed him.

Belief in all that the Scriptures teach about the person and work of the Lord Jesus Christ is the Christian's foundation. On that sure foundation he should build a life consistent with that faith. There are pitfalls all about, but the One who saves will also keep.

For the world, and for the individual,
what a difference it makes . . .

CHARACTER

Fiber is the tough substance that gives texture and body to plants and trees. From it cloth is spun or woven. And it is fiber that makes trees useful for lumber and other products.

In man, character is the fiber that determines behavior and reaction to the strains and stresses of life. It has been said that a man's real character is shown by what he does when he is alone, but that is only part of the picture. Whenever temptations come or pressures rise, and decisions have to be made, character or its lack is very evident.

There is a form of good character that is not necessarily based on the Christian ethic. Until the Red take-over in China, there was evident (and there still is, in Chinese communities abroad) a praiseworthy character rooted in respect for family and a sense of family responsibility. No doubt this is why there is so little crime and delinquency in Chinese communities. Obedience to and honor for parents results in law-abiding character.

When the Communists took over China, one of their first objectives was to destroy the age-long sense of family loyalty, and the day came when children's denunciation of parents was commonplace.

America, which was founded on the Christian ethic, has also experienced a marked decline in character. Now expediency often triumphs over right, and immediate gain is thought by many to justify almost any act. Even among some religious leaders, "situation ethics" has supplanted the absolute of God's moral law. Never has there been greater need for Christian character than now.

We do not have to look far to find what has largely led to the moral and spiritual decline of American life (which is, of course, a reflection of individual lives). The biblical concept of good and evil has been dimmed or lost, and men no longer have the moral fiber necessary to stand up against the multiplied temptations of today. The faith and conviction that form the basis of character have deteriorated. And the values that make men and nations great are under external attack everywhere. On every hand evil is called good and good evil.

If one has no inner standard of values, why should he oppose what is wrong? If one's source of reference is no higher than the behavior of others, he can travel to disaster without ever sensing the danger ahead. Without a God-oriented sense of values, there can be no Christian conscience.

Years ago, when I was a medical student in Richmond, I had the privilege of helping in the Seventeenth Street Mission on Sunday afternoons. One day a young Negro boy was arrested and brought into court. When he was asked, "Did you steal that box?," the little fellow replied: "No sir, Judge, that would be sin."

The bemused judge asked, "What is sin?" He received the immediate answer, "Sin is any want of conformity unto or transgression of the law of God." Needless to say, this case was investigated and the the honesty of the little boy proved beyond doubt. He had character developed by Christian teaching and a loyalty to what he had been taught.

How tragic that so few young people are learning the foundation of Christian character today! Even in many Sunday schools, the development of a strong sense of right and wrong, of man's responsibility to God and the teaching of Scripture, is slighted in favor of development of "social consciousness." The result: anti-social behavior on every hand.

Why are so many people unwilling to "get involved" when others are in trouble, even before their eyes? Because character has been supplanted by selfishness.

Why is there so little righteous indignation against those who are actively destroying the values that made our nation great? Why is there no firm reaction against those who have lost all patriotism and who actively engage in sedition and acts of treason?

Recently a well-known folk-singer was refused the use of an auditorium in Washington because of her encouragement of draftcard-burners and draft-dodgers. The news media made a heroine of her while those who refused the use of their auditorium were held up to ridicule. Could this have been possible without the undermining of the foundations of national conscience by an insidious propaganda that rejects all restraint? "Freedom" has become license, and in that grievous perversion conscienceless men are spelling the doom of a nation.

But there is hope. That hope lies in people who have consciences controlled by the living Christ. One develops such a conscience by becoming thoroughly saturated with the Word of God, by learning to look at the world in the light of God's holy laws.

Let young people read and reread the Book of Proverbs,

for there they will learn the basis for right behavior. Let them receive Christ into their hearts and they will, through the help of the indwelling Spirit, know how to react to temptations and the insidious propaganda of Satan, to which they are constantly subjected.

Young people need to learn of Daniel, whose strong character was reflected in his resolve "not [to] defile himself with the king's rich food, or with the wine which he drank" (Dan. 1:8); of Timothy, to whom Paul wrote, "Take your share of suffering as a good soldier of Christ Jesus" (II Tim. 2:3); and of Isaiah, who could say, "The Lord God helps me; therefore I have not been confounded; therefore I have set my face like a flint, and I know that I shall not be put to shame" (Isa. 50:7).

One step toward developing a God-oriented conscience in America would be to institute the reading of the Ten Commandments each day in all public schools. God's moral law, common to the heritage of Jews, Catholics, and Protestants, read without comment, would be a blessing and help to all, particularly those who have never learned the meaning of right and wrong. If attendance at this reading were made optional, even the mouths of avowed atheists would be stopped.

The American heritage is saturated with the recognition of God and our responsibility to him. How can we continue to permit the frittering away of our most precious possession in the name of a "freedom" that is actually bondage to evil?

If we are to regain the character that once made us great, we *must* have a source of reference—God's holy law, which enables us to distinguish good from evil. When character is founded on Christ and his Word, we see through the blandishments by which we are being led down the path to oblivion.

Christian character, the fiber that makes men and nations great, is desperately needed today. For a generation there has been a growing tendency to let men set the standards with disastrous results. We have forgotten that "righteousness exalts a nation, but sin is a reproach to any people" (Prov. 14:34).

Character makes the difference.

In view of the need, and her calling,
has the Church been . . .

CAUGHT OFF BASE

The "pick off" is one of the most exciting plays in baseball. But it is humiliating for the player who is victim either of the pitcher's expert timing or of his own carelessness in straying too far from base.

The Church is in danger of finding herself the victim of a "pick-off" play, that is, of becoming so wrapped up in secondary or extraneous affairs that she is "out," no longer a part of the game to which her Lord called her.

No one questions the duty of the Church to become "involved"; but she should be very sure of what it is that God has called her to be involved in. Just as a surgeon would prove useless to an ill patient if he spent his time clerking in a haberdashery store, so the Church fails in her primary mission when she becomes involved, as a corporate institution, in social, economic, and political matters, which are outside her jurisdiction and competence.

The pastor of one of America's great churches preached a sermon from which with his permission, we quote extensively, because of its clarity and vital importance. He said:

"What is the primary responsibility of the Church? To preach the Gospel of God's redemption and the renewal of the individual through Jesus Christ, or to reform society? According to the Bible, the Church is basically and inescapably committed to the proclamation of the Gospel. Along with its proclamation of the Gospel message, the Church is, through its redeemed members, obligated to be the salt of the earth.

"For Christians and the Church, the recognition of spiritual and moral sickness is only the beginning and not the end. To be sure, the national and international situation is alarming; but it is not beyond the reach of the Lord of men and nations. It is the glory of the Gospel that Christ came precisely to minister to man's needs. He didn't come to save the righteous but sinners. Flagrant sin, social upheavals, political uncertainties, international tensions abound, but these are only symptoms of the disease Christ came to cure.

"And this message is committed to his Church. Today, many leaders in the Church choose to emphasize 'social engineering,' but it remains the imperative duty of the Church to preach redemption through Christ, and reconciliation to God. For too long some loud ecclesiastical voices have stressed 'social problems' and minimized sin in the human heart. Until this process is reversed, the Church will continue to fail in her primary task.

"Out of this shift in emphasis some strange attitudes to law have emerged. Law, the very basis of an orderly and just society of free men, is openly flouted in the name of 'social justice.'

"There has been altogether too much disrespect for the laws of the land, both in social protest and in the administration of justice. When citizens tolerate, condone, and foster breaking the laws openly, or by non-violent disobedience, they are only undermining the one social structure that can best serve their own causes. The trouble is that non-violence often leads to violence.

"Personally I deplore the participation of some of my fellow ministers who feel it necessary to break just laws or take to the streets in order to register their social convictions in a democratic society. Christian leaders are ill advised when they take the law into their own hands, for whatever reason, or encourage and support others who do so.

"Today, the American people are inviting a flood of riots and rebellion by the cracks they themselves are putting in the dam of their own laws and constitution, by the disrespect for law and order and for the police which many Americans, including preachers, are encouraging.

"Then, too, in the administration of justice, we have become altogether too lenient with law-breakers at all levels. All too often the sympathy of the courts and the religious community seems to be on the side of the criminal. . . . We blame society for creating the criminal—it's never his fault— and we use all manner of excuses and legal loopholes to keep the wrongdoer from being punished.

"Believe you me, as long as this soft policy toward criminals is maintained, there is little hope of conquering the crime wave. History records that many civilizations have been destroyed from within. Let us heed that warning lest we succumb to the tyranny of criminal anarchy.

"Again, we Christians ought to have the common sense to realize that, with all our respect for minorities and provision for minority opinion, our democratic culture is based on the rule of the majority. We seem to have forgotten that majorities have civil rights as well as minorities. . . . The rights of minorities must be respected, of course, except where the exercise of those rights infringes upon the rights of others.

"This applies to many areas other than the race issue.

We see it on university campuses . . . in groups of vocal faculty members . . . in the work of a tiny minority of atheists. . . . Our common sense should tell us that the techniques of agitation and protest by clamorous minorities need to be heavily discounted. . . . Protest has its place in a free country, but it can be carried to extremes. . . .

"Once more, we Christians need the common sense to know that there is nothing wrong with love of country, and that our nation deserves our devotion and support, and that freedom is worth defending against all enemies within and without.

"I am thoroughly convinced that the Christian Church should exert its peculiar power in society as an instrument of God to change the hearts and attitudes of men, and not as a social or economic pressure group or as a legislative body. . . . The Kingdom of God simply can't be equated with the welfare state or the civil rights movement. . . . Just now the Church is in grave peril of an increasing deviation from its divinely assigned task. It is in danger of fanning the flames of futility when it should be earnestly striving to bring individuals to a reconciliation with God, and a saving knowledge of his Son Jesus Christ.

"Let the Church be what God has called it to be—a worshiping community of believers, proclaiming the Gospel of redemption and reconciliation with God, seeking to observe all things its Lord has commanded it. This, and nothing less than this, is what the Church of Jesus Christ is for."

When we consider these clear statements about the mission and the message of the Church, we can see her danger; caught off base because of her preoccupation with secondary matters, because of her shift from her God-ordained responsibility in the things of the Spirit to a primary concern for social matters. Should her proposed social changes and adjustments be made, men outside of Christ would still be lost—without God and without hope.

The Church must not become the victim of the Devil's "pick-off" play.

*They were effective in the past
and today the Church has . . .*

THE SAME TOOLS

The general deterioration of the world situation, the population explosion without a corresponding acceleration in the world's spiritual birthrate, and the seeming loss of spiritual power to be noted among Christians and in the corporate church is causing deep searching of heart by thoughtful Christians. There is a feeling that something must happen to bring a change in the situation.

Some would have the Church become "involved" in the world to such an extent that no distinction would be made between a believer and a non-believer. These feel that Christianity is no longer a force to be reckoned with because it is not relevant to the contemporary world scene. Because the gospel message had its origin in the first century and this is the twentieth, and because the Bible stresses an otherworldly orientation for the Christian that seems unrealistic for our times, there are those who feel the historic, biblically based Christianity of our forefathers is no longer applicable.

On the other hand, many sincere Christians are deeply troubled because the phrase, "the post-Christian era," has a ring of reality that disturbs the soul and shakes confidence in present methods to reach an unbelieving world that is in desperate need.

In considering the theories of those who would reject the present validity of historic Christianity, let us ask a few questions: Are the basic needs of men different now from what they were 2,000 years ago? Or has God's provision for those needs changed? Despite the sophistication of our age and the almost unbelievable advances in science, is man basically different from what he was in the time of Christ?

The human heart was deceitful then and is deceitful today. The lusts of the flesh, the lust of the eyes, and the pride of life continue to grip each new generation. Sophisticated, scientifically advanced, modern in outlook, man is still a sinful creature estranged from God and desperately in need of forgiveness, cleansing, and a new heart.

It was to meet this need that the Son of God came into this world, died, and arose again from the dead. The world has not outgrown its need, nor has the Gospel of God's redemption in Jesus Christ lost its power.

Why then this lapse in effectiveness by the Church and by many Christians? It is unfortunately true that in an age of sophistication, affluence, and a growing understanding and use of scientific discoveries, many now try to convince themselves that they are self-sufficient and do not need God or his Christ.

But men's hearts still yearn for something higher than material things. Strip off the veneer of our civilization and there remains a desperate loneliness, a sense of frustration, a void that remains empty unless it is filled with the living Christ.

We must keep clearly in mind the message of the Church and also the tools of missions and evangelism that God has given us for spreading that message.

To the Church has been given the message of a higher destiny, of a renewed fellowship with God through faith in his Son, of a new life where companionship replaces loneliness and purpose replaces frustration.

One look at this chaotic world and we are ready to throw up our hands in hopelessness. How, we ask ourselves, can the Gospel become a living force in a world so obviously alienated from God? What is needed to recapture the power and the glory of the Gospel for this generation?

Here is where we need to take a new look at the *tools* God has provided. (We use the term "tools" reverently to refer to certain things that God has placed at our disposal, to be used for his glory.)

If we think our world is chaotic and hopeless, what kind of a world did the disciples face in the first century? On every hand there was the entrenched evil of paganism. But apparently the disciples ignored the obstacles because of the tremendous message and the marvelous tools they had. By God's work through them, the message became effective in the lives of men and women in every walk of life, so that in a few short years the then-known world had heard of Jesus Christ, his death, and his resurrection, and enough had believed to change the whole course of history.

This handful of uneducated, ordinary men had irresistible tools, and God worked a miracle. The same tools are available today, but they are too often neglected. In their place men use man-made devices that perish with their makers and those on whom they are used.

The early disciples had been with Jesus, and this personal experience with the risen Lord had transformed them into fervent evangelists. But God never intended that they alone should know Christ as Saviour and Lord. To all of us is given the same privilege, and without it we are useless.

91

It is hardly possible for someone to win men to Jesus Christ who does not know him through personal experience. We all need to have a deep, personal experience of the saving power of Jesus Christ in our hearts and lives.

The early disciples also were imbued with the power of the Holy Spirit. They had been emptied of self, and the Holy Spirit possessed them to the point where God was doing the work and they were simply instruments. Today similar power is waiting for those who give the Holy Spirit his rightful place in their lives and in their work.

The early disciples were also men of prayer. They believed in divine intervention in their problems. They believed that prayer released God's almighty power on behalf of his own and their work for him. When confronted with danger, opposition, and humanly insoluble situations, they turned to God in prayer and he heard and answered.

The early disciples used the Old Testament Scriptures to confirm their preaching. In every case they recognized the Scriptures as finally authoritative. Today we have not only the Old but also the New Testament to use as the invincible Sword of the Spirit.

The early disciples had a message—repentance, forgiveness of sins, and salvation through faith in the risen Lord. This simple and direct message penetrated to the heart of man's need, the same need men have today.

Finally, *the early disciples had no money.* Can it be that part of their success stemmed from their utter dependence on God, rather than on material assets?

Through these men the early Church came into being. Although they lacked much of what we prize most highly, such as education and financial security, they succeeded.

We have the same tools. If we use them faithfully, the world can again be turned upside down for Jesus Christ.

There is no question but that
the Gospel is . . .

SUFFICIENT FOR THE TASK

The church's primary task is to evangelize the world, to preach Christ at home and abroad. But while the need continues, the present-day counsel of defeatism and gloom is taking its toll.

The population explosion, which has led to a rapid increase in the number of unbelievers, and the lethargy caused by a growing universalism that salves consciences and blunts the sense of urgency in mission are among the factors now having a great effect upon Christians and the Church. Many of us are overwhelmed by the magnitude of the task and the indifference and sophistication of an age in which a growing number feel that God and his Gospel are at best of secondary importance.

We need to take stock, first, of our obligation to preach the Gospel to all nations, and then of the assets at our disposal. Once this is done, pessimism will be replaced by confidence in God's promises, and lagging attempts will be turned to Spirit-inspired activity.

Christians need to be realistic. They should heed our Lord's

93

command and be sensitive to the needs of a generation far removed from a knowledge of Christ.

The world might be likened to a person with a dislocated joint. The joint is painful, and its function is lost. Spiritually dislocated from God, the world is confused and frustrated because it knows neither the cause nor the cure of its suffering. Many persons I knew as a missionary in China tried to treat a dislocation with a poultice of pitch; and the world's attempts to solve its problems without considering God are just as mistaken and futile.

This is where the Church comes into the picture, and she should give herself to the task of healing with unabated zeal. Instead of trying to relieve symptoms, however, she should see the cause and proclaim the God-given cure.

But let us be realistic. Is not the task too great? Are not the obstacles too numerous? Are we not too weak to bring about a change that can be effective against the overwhelming odds?

After Pentecost a handful of men, most of them uneducated and probably unprepossessing, went out to preach, and in a few generations the world was turned upside down for Christ.

What did they have that we do not have? Why was their witness so effective? They were a tiny minority confronted by the hostility of the Jews and the ridicule of the pagan Gentiles. But men were converted, the Church was established, and Christians helped bring about tremendous social changes. Did these uneducated and ordinary men have something we have lost, or perhaps have failed to use?

We have the same assests today. And we will be just as effective as the early disciples if we use them.

These men had an aura about them. They had been with

Jesus, and they carried in their hearts and on their faces the sign of redeemed men, men who had had a personal experience with the risen Saviour. They had had the privilege of seeing, talking with, and even touching the One who they knew had been crucified and buried. Through simple faith we can have the same experience. Christ can be as real to us as he was to them, and transform our lives.

We have *the same God* these men had. He may be dead for those who have never known him, but we know that he lives and that by his grace we too live. We know him personally, and we are aware of his promise to be with us, even to the end of the age.

He is the God of whom the psalmist said, "from everlasting to everlasting thou art God" (Ps. 90:2c, RSV). He is the One of whom Isaiah wrote, "The Lord is the everlasting God, the Creator of the ends of the earth. He does not faint or grow weary, his understanding is unsearchable" (Isa. 40:28). He is the "Father of lights in whom there is no variation or shadow due to change" (Jas. 1:17).

We have *the same risen Lord.* The resurrection was an ever-recurring theme in the preaching of the disciples. Christ had risen from the dead, and his resurrection was the crowning proof of the validity of the Cross. How much do we stress this fact? Have we permitted the scientific approach of our day to blunt the belief that we have a supernatural religion that *naturally* has supernatural manifestations? Is our God so small that we look at him through a test tube, or seek answers about him from a computer?

We have *the same Gospel,* which the Apostle Paul said is "the power of God for salvation to everyone who has faith" (Rom. 1:16). It is the same gospel that Paul summed up in the wonderfully simple and clear statement, ". . . that Christ died for our sins in accordance with the scriptures, that he was buried, that he was raised on the third day in accordance with

95

the scriptures" (I Cor. 15:3, 4). It is the same Gospel that today brings conviction, conversion, and redemption whenever and wherever it is preached—not to all men (nor did it in our Lord's time) but to all who heed the Spirit's call.

We have *the same Holy Spirit,* the One who was the power behind the apostles' preaching and who is able and willing to make our preaching and teaching effective if only we will place programs, organizations, personalities, and activities in their rightful secondary place. The disciples were commanded to stay in Jerusalem until the Holy Spirit came upon them and they were baptized with his power; this was the equipment necessary for fulfilling the Lord's command to make disciples of all nations. Our failures today stem largely from our forgetting that it is "not by might, nor by power, but by my Spirit, says the Lord of hosts" (Zech. 4:6).

We have *the same Holy Scriptures,* which continue to be the Sword of the Spirit wherever used and believed. The difference today is that we have a fuller revelation of divine truth than did the early disciples. They had only the Old Testament, and to this they referred for authority and for what they knew to be divine truth. We have the Old *and* the New Testaments, in which is revealed the Christ, faith in whom has brought salvation to all who believe.

We have *the same privilege and power of prayer*—direct communication with the throne of grace, where there is help, guidance, and blessing for all who seek it.

Since we, like those men who went out to shake the world for Jesus Christ, have all these assets, why has the cause of world evangelization lagged? The inevitable conclusion is that we are not making use of what God has provided. Weak in faith, distracted by world conditions, sophisticated to the point of disdaining the simplicity of the first-century approach (sometimes even feeling, perhaps, that we need not heed our Lord's command to preach the Gospel to all nations because "people are already saved"), we are guilty of disobedience, or of unwillingness to give our all to Christ and go out as he commanded to tell men that Christ has the answer to personal needs as well as those of the entire world.

It can be done. With the assets we have from God, it can be done.

Be sure you keep time
(and times) accurately . . .

NOT NINETEENTH—FIRST

Until recently it was popular to make light of the evangelical approach to the Gospel by referring to it as "seventeenth-century Christianity, not relevant to the twentieth century." Now the charge has advanced a bit; ours is a "nineteenth-century message, outdated by the space age."

We will be wise to keep things in perspective by being aware of what was relevant in the first century after Christ and what is relevant now.

In the first century, when the Gospel was first preached, what did men need?

To put it in the simplest terms possible, they needed a revelation of God, changed hearts, a new dynamic for living, and a hope for the future.

What was the need of the social order when the Gospel was first preached?

The social order, composed of men and women, desperately needed redeemed people to bring into play a new ethic, supplanting the tyranny of power and lust by the fruits of the Spirit.

The social order of the first century needed to be confronted with its own insufficiency, for neither the culture and philosophers of Greece nor the power of Rome with her dedication to law and order was able to cope with the problems caused by sin in the human heart.

Today men and nations, the politician and the philosopher, the ignorant and the sophisticated—all have the same needs as did those who lived nineteen centuries ago.

If, then, man's need today is the same as it was when men first went out to preach the Gospel, the burning question is whether the Gospel of the first century is relevant for the twentieth.

What was that Gospel?

That all men are sinners, standing under the judgment of God; that the wages of sin is death; that God loves all men everywhere; and that he has made full provision for the sin problem in the death and resurrection of his Son. Paul telescoped the Gospel in these words: ". . . that Christ died for our sins in accordance with the scriptures, that he was buried, that he was raised on the third day in accordance with the scriptures" (I Cor. 15:3h, 4, RSV).

The basic need of man for personal salvation is brushed aside only through a rejection of the clear record of Scripture. To suggest that the space age has changed the hearts of men is utter foolishness. A reading of any newspaper reveals that the hearts of men are still desperately wicked.

To admit the diagnosis but then turn to education, power politics, or social engineering for the solution is to add folly to folly.

To say that the industrial, atomic, or space age represents problems that first-century Christianity is unable to solve is to limit the power of God and to imply that scientific, sophisticated man needs a God not revealed in the Gospel of the first century.

Part of the problem is the confusing of God's message of redemption with *methods* of making that message known. For a Christian to insist on traveling as Paul traveled, or limiting himself to the means of communication available in Paul's time, would be an absurdity. As each generation comes into its responsibility of preaching the Gospel, it should make use of every new means for making Christ known. People must be reached where they are, not where we wish they were. Each generation of Christians must speak to the heart hunger of the multitudes with the tenderness and love found only in the hearts of those who have been touched by the Master.

Preaching the Gospel in the twentieth century requires, as always, consecrated common sense. To think that the social order can be changed without changing the hearts of the people who compose that social order is perhaps the least realistic concept imaginable. In fact, it is downright foolishness.

Those who preached the Gospel message in the first century did not gloss over man's condition and need. When our Lord commissioned the Apostle Paul as a minister to his generation, he said, "I send you to open their eyes, that they may turn from darkness to light and from the power of Satan to God, that they may receive forgiveness of sins and a place among those who are sanctified by faith in me" (Acts 26:18).

What was the condition of those to whom Paul was commissioned to preach, and what was his message to be?

Men are *spiritually blind* until their eyes are opened by the Holy Spirit. Are men in the twentieth century more spiritually enlightened than their brothers in the first? Only by faith in Christ were men's eyes opened then, and this remains true today. Men out of Christ—in the jungles of

Ecuador and in the most sophisticated universities—are still living in spiritual darkness.

Men in the first century were *under the power of Satan.* What conceivable evidence is there today that those who do not know the Saviour are any less under that power? It is popular to deny the reality of Satan, but it is exceedingly difficult to deny the evidence of his activity.

To turn men from the power of Satan to God was a work of personal conversion that men needed in Paul's time and that they need today. The imperative. "Ye must be born again," has never been invalidated.

By the Gospel men could receive *forgiveness of sins.* All through the Acts of the Apostles we hear the plea to *repent.* Do men need "repentance to God and faith in our Lord Jesus Christ" (Acts 20:21) less today than they did then? Are we not living in a generation that is sinning far more against the light than did those people in Paul's time? Are we cloaking our rejection of personal repentance for sins by calling for "corporate repentance for corporate sins" instead? We need personal forgiveness by the One who alone can forgive our sins.

Paul was commissioned to preach a Gospel that would bring sanctification—*a new life*—by faith in Jesus Christ. The risen Lord knew the hearts of men. He knew their needs in the first century. Men have not changed. Their hearts are the same, "desperately wicked," and their need for personal salvation continues.

Men make all sorts of desperate efforts to substitute something else for the first-century Gospel. The shrinking world, growth of cults, resurgence of pagan religions, population explosion, lessening influence of the Church—all are used as an excuse to change the Gospel to something more palatable to unregenerate man.

What is advanced by some today as "twentieth-century Christianity" is not Christianity at all. It is a gospel of accommodation to man, not the Gospel of man's reconciliation to God through faith in his Son.

Men may change the method of preaching and teaching the Gospel and thereby be more effective in the twentieth century. But woe unto them—and to those deceived by them —if they change the Gospel Paul preached and the commission he received from his Lord on the road to Damascus!

God forbid that we should be deceived by a form of godliness that denies the power by which alone we are redeemed.

Here is a legitimate question . . .

HOW BIG IS GOD?

Those who have a low concept of God have rejected the multiplied revelations he has given of himself—in his works of creation and providence, in the person of his Son, in the presence of his Spirit, and in his written Word. He has not left himself without a witness, and the evidence demands that we worship and praise the One thus revealed.

God is *infinite*—without limits of any kind. Limited as we are by time, space, and circumstances, we find it difficult even to apprehend dimly the fact that for God there are no such limitations. As Solomon said, "heaven, even highest heaven, cannot contain him" (II Chron. 2:6*b*, RSV). The psalmist affirms, "Great is the Lord, and abundant in power; his understanding is beyond measure" (Ps. 147:5).

God is *omnipotent*—all powerful, the master of every situation. Jesus said, "With God all things are possible" (Matt. 19:26*b*). Some day every Christian will hear the proclamation, "Hallelujah! the Lord God omnipotent reigneth" (Rev. 19:6*b*, KJV).

God is *omniscient;* he always knows all of the past, the

present, and the future. Eternity lies before him like a vast panorama. Nothing is hidden from his knowledge.

God is *omnipresent;* there is no place where man can escape his presence. David expressed this in Psalm 139. Truly there is no place where man can hide. Outer space, the depths of the ocean, darkness—all are alike to him. "Even the darkness is not dark to thee, the night is bright as the day; for darkness is as light with thee" (Ps. 139:12).

God is *sovereign.* Even in the chaos of today's world, he is working out his holy purposes; and they will certainly be fulfilled. Who is man to question the wisdom or sovereign power of God?

We learn something of the nature of God when we pray, "For thine is the kingdom, and the power, and the glory, for ever." We affirm that his kingdom is eternal, that his power is infinite, and that his glory encompasses infinite love, holiness, justice, and mercy. And we affirm that these things are for ever.

God is all this and more. He is the *Creator* of all things seen and unseen, of the laws that govern the universe, of the perfections in evidence on every hand in nature.

What folly, then, for the creature to question or doubt the Creator! The Apostle Paul pointedly asks, "Who are you, a man, to answer back to God? Will what is molded say to its molder, 'Why have you made me thus?'" (Rom. 9:20).

Nothing is more humbling than to contemplate the infinite power and wisdom evinced in God's works of creation. "The heavens are telling the glory of God; and the firmament proclaims his handiwork" (Ps. 19:1). Only the spiritually blind can fail to see the greatness and the glory of God in his creation.

God is not only the Creator; he is also the *Redeemer,* returning to the world he made to redeem sinning man back to himself. Exercising his right of choice, man disobeyed God; and sin brought separation. But the love of God would not permit man to continue in a hopeless state. God came in the person of his Son so that once more man could choose and those who believed could be redeemed.

Not only did God create, not only does he redeem, he also *preserves* by his works of providence. The amazing fact that all things work out for the good of God's children—any possible circumstance of life—is an evidence of his preserving and overruling power. How can we fail to worship such a God!

Yet, despite his majesty, power, and wisdom, God is the God of the individual. He is a *personal* God to all who receive him. To reject him means chaos in every aspect of life.

He is concerned with the great problems and minute details of our lives.

O, what peace we often forfeit,
O, what needless pain we bear,
All because we do not carry
Everything to God in prayer.

This is not the figment of a pious imagination; it is the statement of a deep and abiding truth.

The psalmist says, "When the cares of my heart are many, thy consolations cheer my soul" (Ps. 94:19). What a loss for those who do not know the privilege of trusting the heavenly Father who is concerned about our personal problems, the Saviour who understands our personal temptations and delivers from them, the Holy Spirit, who is a personal Comforter to those who turn to him! How truly David spoke when he said, "The Lord is my shepherd." This was a personal relationship for life, for death, and for all eternity.

How big is God? He is the *God of destiny*. It is he who determines the outcome of history and who stands in the shadows keeping watch over his own.

Men and nations may parade grandly across the stage of history, but they do not determine the course of either life or death. The curtain of history will be drawn, not by man, but by God.

How big is God? Look about you and see the evidence of his wisdom and power. If a man claims to be an artist, one has the right to ask to see his pictures. If he says he is an architect, one wants to see something he has designed; if an athlete, to see his prowess; if an inventor, to see his product.

Look at the heavens, the moon and the stars. Look at the earth, all the marvels of God's creative power. Look at his Son and Calvary. Look in his Word and all it reveals. Look into the innermost reaches of your troubled soul and hear him speak peace. You will get an inkling of how great he is.

How big is God? He can never be measured by earthly standards, but on every hand we see signs of his glory. God is a spirit, and we can grasp what this means only when we worship him in spirit and in truth. Although he is nearer than hands or feet, yet he encompasses all of time and eternity.

Staggering? Of course. But, oh, how comforting to those who know him!

God's witness is *universal*, to be seen and known by all who will. It is *continuing*, from one generation to another. It is *personal;* he stands at the door of the human heart, knocking and seeking admittance.

Moses knew this when he said, "Lord, thou has been our dwelling place in all generations. Before the mountains were brought forth, or ever thou hadst formed the earth and the world, from everlasting to everlasting thou art God" (Ps. 90:1, 2).

Man may try to limit God by his own earthbound limitations. He may blaspheme God by saying he is dead. He may defy God by conspiring against him. But "he who sits in the heavens laughs; the Lord has them in derision" (Ps. 2:4). Some day all who have limited him or blasphemed or conspired against him will find to their eternal horror what a "fearful thing" it is "to fall into the hands of the living God," "for our God is a consuming fire" (Heb. 10:31, 12:29).

God has set before us an array of witnesses, inanimate and animate, that combine to tell us as much as the human mind can grasp of infinity. Jesus tells us where faith enters the picture: "Unless you turn and become like children, you will never enter the kingdom of heaven" (Matt. 18:3).

Recognize who He is . . .

SPARRING WITH GOD

Spectacular crimes often are followed by widely publicized trials. Some of the defense techniques are repeated in one form or another again and again. The accused may have been seen in the act of committing murder. He may have been apprehended immediately. There is no doubt as to the guilt of the accused.

But the defense is clever: "He was not responsible for his actions at the moment when he fired the fatal shot," or, "He was temporarily deranged because of alcohol or some other drug," or, "His thinking was blurred and motivation confused; therefore, he should not be held personally responsible for his actions."

In all of this we are witnessing a certain legal technique. The lawyers for the defense are sparring with the court. They use every possible means to confuse the jury and to interpose technicalities in favor of their client. This is accepted practice. It is the means whereby some innocent victims of circumstances are protected, and whereby many who are guilty receive less punishment than their crimes may deserve.

What is permissible with man, however, is not necessarily

permissible with God. Techniques contrived to deliver man from the clutches of the law are of no avail against the Judge of the universe. One may spar with the courts of the land, but to try to do so when dealing with God is futile.

And yet, man is ever prone to make excuses for himself. He ignores the solemn warning, "Woe to him who strives with his Maker, an earthen vessel with the potter!" (Isa. 45:9).

Let's be honest and face up to the situation. Let us be prepared to accept God's diagnosis of the condition of the human heart: "For the heart is deceitful above all things, and desperately corrupt; who can understand it? 'I the Lord search the mind and try the heart'" (Jer. 17:9, 10a).

Let us admit that we cannot fool God, "for the Lord sees not as man sees; man looks on the outward appearance, but the Lord looks on the heart" (I Sam. 16:7b). The all-seeing and all-knowing God cannot be hoodwinked: "Before him no creature is hidden, but all are open and laid bare to the eyes of him with whom we have to do" (Heb. 4:13).

And our Lord puts his finger squarely on the source and nature of the evil of which all are guilty: "For from within, out of the heart of man, come evil thoughts, fornication, theft, murder, adultery, coveting, wickedness, deceit, licentiousness, envy, slander, pride, foolishness. All these evil things come from within, and they defile a man" (Mark 7:21–23).

What a catalogue of the sins of the flesh and spirit! Who can deny his own guilt? Who can ignore the fact that *all is known to God?*

The guilt is established. And the penalty is clearly stated: "Death!"

What can a man do under these circumstances? He can deny his guilt, but God is aware of it. He can say the penalty is too severe, but he is dealing with a holy God, not imperfect man and his courts. He can shrug off his guilt and say that he is not responsible for his actions, that his parents are to blame, or his environment is responsible, but there comes the haunting echo: "So they are without excuse" (Rom. 1:20b).

What is there to do?

Confess! Throw yourself on the mercy of the court! Don't lie to the Judge. "If we say we have no sin, we deceive ourselves, and the truth is not in us. If we confess our sins, he is faithful and just, and will forgive our sins and cleanse us from all unrighteousness" (I John 1:8, 9).

God honors a candid confession of sin. No sins are so black as to take him by surprise; he already knows all about them. When for the sake of our eternal soul we make a clean breast of everything, an amazing thing happens: The Holy Spirit intercedes for us. The Judge becomes our Advocate and comes down from the judgment seat to take our part. We find ourselves innocent because the One whose laws we have broken has already paid the penalty for us.

This is the greatest news in all the world. It is the Gospel of the Lord Jesus Christ, and *he has given his word and his life* to make it true.

Why are so many silent about these things? The fact of sin in the world is something all can see. The reality of sin in our own hearts is as real as our breathing and heartbeat. Accepting Jesus' words about the condition of the human heart and the sins that proceed from it, we should stand convicted in our own consciences. It is I who stand guilty in the court of the Most High God.

The wonder of it all is that the very one whose holy laws we have broken has paid for us the penalty and taken from us the guilt. With the Apostle Paul we can shout, "If God is for us, who can be against us?" (Rom. 8:31b).

How can man, a sinner by nature and a sinner by practice, learn to judge this world and his own actions in the light of God's holiness? Is God not so remote that man finds himself groping when he needs light?

There is a sure way to distinguish good from evil. The test of the Holy Scriptures. "For the word of God is living and active, sharper than any two-edged sword, piercing to the division of soul and spirit, of joints and marrow, and discerning the thoughts and intentions of the heart" (Heb. 4:12).

Like a searchlight, the Bible shows us the remote corners of our lives, revealing things we would like so much to hide. Like an X-ray, the Scriptures penetrate into the innermost being until we are able to see things from God's perspective. Like a surgeon's knife, the written Word of God lays bare the thoughts, motives, subterfuges, and lies we conceal from men. How revealing that the verse in Hebrews 4 quoted above is followed immediately by the sobering statement, "And before him no creature is hidden, but all are open and laid bare to the eyes of him with whom we have to do." It is the King of kings with whom we have to do. We stand before him guilty and condemned. But the situation can be changed in the twinkling of an eye. When a sinner casts himself on the mercy of the court, he is turning to the One who is altogether merciful.

A trembling prisoner, when he was told, "Don't worry, you will get justice," replied, "What I need is not justice but mercy." The sinner can plead the Name of Jesus Christ, knowing that with him there is mercy, and also redemption.

Let no man deceive you with the devil's lie—that you are a pretty good chap and that God is so loving and kind he will never condemn anyone. Jesus tells us that "he who does not believe is condemned already, because he has not believed in the name of the only Son of God" (John 3:18).

God "too loving to condemn"? It is because he loved so

much that he sent his Son into the world to give everlasting life to those who in simple faith believe in him.

To spar with God may seem intellectually stimulating—but it is done at the risk of eternal damnation.

All around you see . . .

THE WITNESS OF CREATION

Truths in the Bible that we read about for years may suddenly burst upon us like a blinding ray of light. I experienced this when I realized that from beginning to end of the Holy Scriptures we are told again and again that the God with whom we have to do is the Creator of all things. This fact that God is the Creator appears some five hundred times.

The Bible opens with these majestic words, "In the beginning God created the heavens and the earth" (Gen. 1:1). And at the end of the Revelation we read: "Then I saw a new heaven and a new earth; for the first heaven and the first earth had passed away, and the sea was no more. . . . And he who sat upon the throne said, 'Behold, I make all things new.' Also he said, 'Write this, for these words are trustworthy and true'" (Rev. 21:1, 5).

Man's first encounter was with the God of creation. His final time-bound encounter will be with the same God, who will make all things new.

Between these two extremes of human history God reminds us again and again that he is the God of creation, and is sovereign in all things. The witness to God in creation is continuous; for every generation it is new each morning and fresh each evening.

God has endowed man with the ability to reason, to evaluate evidence, and to come to logical conclusions. All around there is the evidence of God's wisdom and power—in creation as a whole, and in the intricacies of its components in particular. David's Spirit-directed observation speaks to our sophisticated age: "The heavens are telling the glory of God; and the firmament proclaims his handiwork. Day to day pours forth speech, and night to night declares knowledge. There is no speech, nor are there words; their voice is not heard; yet their voice goes out through all the earth, and their words to the end of the world" (Ps. 19:1–4).

To even the dullest mind there should come the realization that these things did not just happen. No combination of fortuitous circumstances could possibly account for the universe, or its component parts. That man has tried to explain away the absolute necessity for a Creator is a sign not of mature reasoning but of willful rejection of facts in favor of theories.

The Apostle Paul speaks with finality about the incontrovertible evidences of Creation: "For what can be known about God is plain to them, because God has shown it to them. Ever since the creation of the world his invisible nature, namely, his eternal power and deity, has been clearly perceived in the things that have been made. So they are without excuse; for although they knew God they did not honor him as God or give thanks to him, but they became futile in their thinking and their senseless minds were darkened. Claiming to be wise, they became fools. . . . They changed the truth about God for a lie and worshiped and served the creature rather than the Creator . . ." (Rom. 1:19–22, 25).

The Prophet Isaiah pleads with a rebellious and sinful

114

Israel, "Have you not known? Have you not heard? The LORD is the everlasting God, the Creator of the ends of the earth. He does not faint or grow weary, his understanding is unsearchable" (Isa. 40:28). Creation implies sovereignty. We read: "Let them praise the name of the LORD! For he commanded and they [sun, moon, and stars, heavens and waters] were created" (Ps. 148:5).

Speaking through the Prophet Jeremiah, God says, "It is I who by my great power and my outstretched arm have made the earth, with the men and animals that are on the earth, and I give it to whomever it seems right to me" (Jer. 27:5). God rightfully claims sovereignty, as the Source of all things, and his creation stands as a continuing and inescapable witness to himself.

The idolatry in which Israel had become involved brought out this challenge: "Thus shall you say to them: 'The gods who did not make the heavens and the earth shall perish from the earth and from under the heavens.' It is he who made the earth by his power, who established the world by his wisdom, and by his understanding stretched out the heavens" (Jer. 10:11, 12).

Affirming his sovereignty as Creator, God repeatedly claims loving obedience from man, his highest creation. But he does more than that. The Creator of all things has come into his creation as Saviour and Lord. That it was to Jesus Christ, the Son of God, that the work of creation was committed is one of the most thrilling parts of divine revelation.

We find the Apostle John saying: "All things were made through him, and without him was not anything made that was made. . . . He was in the world, and the world was made through him, yet the world knew him not" (John 1:3, 10). Paul takes up the same theme: "Yet for us there is one God, the Father, from whom are all things and for whom we exist,

115

and one Lord Jesus Christ, through whom are all things and through whom we exist" (I Cor. 8:6). Again Paul says: "For in him all things were created in heaven and on earth, visible and invisible, whether thrones or dominions or principalities or authorities—all things were created through him and for him. He is before all things, and in him all things hold together" (Col. 1:16, 17). The writer of the Epistle to the Hebrews likewise confirms the stupendous fact that God the Creator and God the Redeemer are one: "In many and various ways God spoke of old to our fathers by the prophets; but in these last days he has spoken to us by a Son, whom he appointed the heir of all things, through whom also he created the world" (Heb. 1:1, 2).

When we are confronted with the witness of creation, our God-given reason demands that we recognize that there must be a Creator, and in the fullness of time he was revealed in the person of God's Son. We experience through our senses the infinite wisdom and power of God the Creator, while in the person of Christ we see his love and redeeming grace.

But in the midst of the perfection of God's creation we also see at work a malignant power, Satan, and his design for evil—so terrible, not only in execution but also in effect, that the Creator's entry into the world became imperative, as an act not only of divine love but also of holy judgment.

God's work of creation is not finished. What we now see will pass away to be replaced by a new heaven and a new earth in which righteousness will prevail. In the interim between the first and second creation God is creating new men through faith in his Son, so that through this spiritual rebirth they may become a part of his eternal Kingdom.

This is not a fanciful concept. It is a part of the divine revelation given in the Scriptures. Not only should we be aware of God's original creation, but we should believe in

Jesus Christ through whose atoning work we may partake of the second creation.

In loving condescension the Creator stands at the door of our heart and knocks. Finally he will ring down the curtain of human history, and that time may be nearer than we think.

Of course, God is Love, but let
all men beware,
He is also capable of . . .

HOLY WRATH

The magnitude of God's Love can be understood only when measured by the extent of his holy wrath against sin. His grace must be seen against the certainty of judgment, his mercy in relation to that from which we have been saved.

We demean the nature and extent of God's love unless we recognize sin for what it is—with its wages, now and for eternity. The Gospel is perverted if God is regarded as a sentimental being to whom men's sins are merely offenses against one another, a matter requiring social reformation only and not redemption and a new creation.

Primarily sin is a matter not of man's inhumanity to man but rather of man's offenses against the holiness of God— human rebellion against divine sovereignty.

Until we are humbled before the love, mercy, and grace of God so that we cry out to him like the lepers of Israel, "Unclean, unclean," we have never even sensed the wonder of salvation. Out of this awareness of God's holiness and our own sinfulness there come true worship, praise, and adoration, and from it there have come some of the world's greatest hymns.

But the man who considers himself worthy of God's love stands condemned by his own pride and folly. Furthermore, any conception of the Gospel solely in terms of service to others is not Christian but humanistic.

Why is this so important? Because of the very nature of God himself, of sin, of man, and of the salvation that is ours through faith in Jesus Christ.

The Bible tells us that "God is love." It also tells us that "our God is a consuming fire" (Heb. 12:29) and that "it is a fearful thing to fall into the hands of the living God" (Heb. 10:31). This seems to be a contradiction. How can both descriptions be true? The answer is found in God's love for the sinner and his wrath against sin.

There are those who decry the concept of an angry God, but there is no other way to explain the Cross. God's holy anger is directed against sin, because of its nature and its effect on mankind. In the wake of the sin of disobedience and rebellion flows a stream of sorrow and suffering, of human ills and spiritual death. God's love required a holy justice offered to all men vicariously in the death of his Son.

But man's contempt for the provision of God's love ends in fearful judgment: "A man who has violated the law of Moses dies without mercy at the testimony of two or three witnesses. How much worse punishment do you think will be deserved by the man who has spurned the Son of God, and profaned the blood of the covenant by which he was sanctified, and outraged the Spirit of grace?" (Heb. 10:28, 29). And after this solemn warning we are told that "it is a fearful thing to fall into the hands of the living God."

Because of the nature of sin and the depravity and weakness of the human heart, God had to take desperate measures. He sent his own Son to give man a glorious alternative to "perishing," which is the offer of eternal life. Our Lord preached the heart of the Gospel in one short statement about God's love for the world and the sending of his Son: "that whoever believes in him should not perish but have eternal life" (John 3:16b).

Why, oh why, has the Gospel been perverted by many into something that hardly resembles its revelation of both the love and wrath of God? The Cross represents an act of redemption, not condemnation: "For God sent the Son into the world, not to condemn the world, but that the world might be saved through him. He who believes in him is not condemned; he who does not believe is condemned already, because he has not believed in the name of the only Son of God" (John 3:17, 18).

God is not an angry God demanding justice. He is a holy God who has provided both justice and salvation. He is a holy God who hates sin enough to provide for man an escape from the condemnation under which he stands.

In the Second Psalm the writer describes the revolt of men and nations against God and speaks of the derisive laughter in heaven that is the prelude to God's righteous judgment. The psalm ends with these words, "Now therefore, O kings, be wise; be warned, O rulers of the earth. . . . Blessed are all who take refuge in him" (Ps. 2:10, 11).

The wrath of God is a devastating reality. And his love is a glorious truth, the depths of which can never be plumbed. The Gospel of redemption in Jesus Christ can be understood only within this context.

There is no escape from the paradoxical doctrines of wrath and love in the assertion that the God of the Old Testament and the God of the New are not the same. They *are* the same God, and some of the strongest denunciations of sinners to be found in all the Bible occur in the New Testament.

The Apostle Paul speaks of the final day when the Lord

suddenly appears in glory: "God deems it just to repay with affliction those who afflict you, and to grant rest with us to you who are afflicted, when the Lord Jesus is revealed from heaven with his mighty angels in flaming fire, inflicting vengeance upon those who do not know God and upon those who do not obey the gospel of our Lord Jesus. They shall suffer the punishment of eternal destruction and exclusion from the presence of the Lord and from the glory of his might" (II Thess. 1:6-9).

There is little comfort here for those who deny that a day will come when Jesus Christ shall be revealed, to judge the unbeliever and take those who have believed to be with him for eternity.

God's wrath is a holy wrath against the spiritually naked—those who have refused to wear the robe of righteousness offered by Christ. It is directed not only against willful unbelief but against all the works of Satan, and Satan himself. It is he who is the arch deceiver, the tempter. And someday this one who lifts his head in pride against almighty God will be cast into the eternal fires of judgment. So too all who resist God, in the pride of human understanding and achievement, stand in danger of his wrath and judgment.

Today all men continue under the eyes of the One who loves them and who in winsomeness says "Come." But the day of wrath will surely come. The Prophet Jeremiah speaks to us today: "To whom shall I speak and give warning, that they may hear? Behold, their ears are closed, they cannot listen; behold, the word of the LORD is to them an object of scorn, they take no pleasure in it. Therefore I am full of the wrath of the LORD, I am weary of holding it in" (Jer. 6:10, 11a).

God loves. He also *warns:* "Your wickedness will chasten

121

you, and your apostasy will reprove you. Know and see that it is evil and bitter for you to forsake the LORD your God; the fear of me is not in you, says the Lord God of hosts" (Jer. 2:19).

It is only right that man should . . .

SEARCH FOR TRUTH

A few months ago a boy examining the stones in an abandoned mine found a ruby worth about $7,000. This gem had been overlooked by thousands who had searched there for something of value.

Man, engaged in his unending "search for truth," continually passes by truth and picks up baubles instead.

Truth has to do with ultimate questions and answers, rather than merely with knowledge and information. Advances in knowledge stagger the imagination. It is estimated that man is prepared to make use of only 10 per cent of the information available to him. Truth has to do with the nature of man—who he is, why he exists, what his destiny is. Truth has to do with God, with good and evil, with sin and redemption, with time and eternity.

And all the while, as men blindly search, Jesus Christ, the Son of God, stands ready to reveal himself as "the Way, the Truth, and the Life" only to be rejected in favor of substitutes that at best leave emptiness in the soul.

Perhaps some of us have been fighting the battle for truth

on the wrong front. We are concerned because of the world's confusion, reflected in every area of life and highlighted by the revolt of young people. Because of our assurance that Christ is the answer for all these problems, we are inclined to wage the battle at the level of doctrines that have to do with his person and work, and with the record of these truths in the inspired and authoritative Scriptures.

But while our own faith and hope rest squarely on Christ, as revealed in the Scriptures, we find that the questions many are asking today delve behind the revelation of God in Jesus Christ to the very existence of God himself.

We are confronted with a generation characterized by ignorance of the Scriptures and the Christ they reveal. It is a generation largely devoid of Bible-based moral and spiritual values, one that has been brought up on a syncretistic philosophical conglomeration where "religion" is, at best, a questionable option.

This spiritually starved generation is to be pitied, because we, of a former generation, have so poorly taught and lived the faith we have professed. In a sense they are like children who are being taught calculus and trigonometry without knowing the multiplication table.

How can Christians help others to find truth? Pious phrases, platitudes, and clichés are meaningless. In these times of spiritual ignorance it is the Spirit who teaches through the Word of God, which is still the Sword of the Spirit, and through lives filled with his presence.

Deep down in the human heart—yes, even in the hearts of a cynical and disillusioned generation—there is a longing for God that can never be satisfied until he is found in the person of his Son, the Lord Jesus Christ.

Although men do not "reason" themselves to God and at some time must take the *unreasonable* step of faith, still we

124

know that God has not left himself without a witness in this world.

As I write I can look out and *see* all around evidences of his hand in creation. I see the sky with clouds scudding across the blue of infinite space; I see trees and flowers and grass; and I, as one who is aware of and believes in the divine revelation, remember that "in the beginning God created the heavens and the earth." I sense the wonder in the words: "The heavens are telling the glory of God; and the firmament proclaims his handiwork. Day to day pours forth speech, and night to night declares knowledge." And I go further, for I know that it was through Jesus Christ that all this was brought into existence: "all things were made through him, and without him was not anything made that was made."

For anyone to think that things just "happen," or that natural objects have within themselves the forces that explain the marvelously intricate operations of the universe, he must exercise a credulity far more difficult than faith.

A scientist searches for facts wherever they may be. He projects hypotheses into the unknown, experiments, gains evidence from multiplied sources or even by accident. But along the way are the evidences of God's handiwork, whether he recognizes them or not. There can be no real and lasting conflict between the facts of science and those of revealed Christianity.

The philosopher, too, if objective in his search, will find in the books of Job and Romans (to mention but two places in the Bible) a depth of philosophical truth that, when illuminated by the Holy Spirit, will transcend anything to be found in the writings of the greatest secular thinkers.

No matter how earnestly a man may search, he is rewarded only when he is willing to accept truth as truth. Honest search will find honest answers, and honesty demands humility, a humility that discards presuppositions in favor of facts.

The greatest single deterrent to man's discovery of truth is the tendency to give precedence to presuppositions that rule out the supernatural and the miraculous. Many "thinkers" today have stumbled over their own doubts to the place where they are blind to God's truth.

Looking for truth, one can look at the universe and be convinced that some rational, powerful, wise, and good Being *must* have brought it into existence. Logic demands that we reject the idea that it is "self-contained," "self-controlled," or "self-developing." The order and wisdom to be found in the universe demands that we accept the fact of a Creator-God.

Let the honest searcher for truth continue his search and he comes face to face with Jesus Christ, the Son of God. The Apostle Paul urges: "See to it that no one makes a prey of you by philosophy and empty deceit, according to human tradition, according to the elemental spirits of the universe, and not according to Christ. For in him the whole fullness of deity dwells bodily" (Col. 2:8, 9).

Searching for truth is not enough. One must recognize it when it is found.

And there is a tragic alternative. One may reject the truth in favor of a lie. Satan is the master counterfeiter, and nowhere is he more active than in the minds of men.

The Apostle Paul describes the evidences God has given of himself in his creation (Rom. 1:19, 20) and then goes on to describe the folly of those who willfully reject this evidence: "Claiming to be wise, they become fools" (v. 22).

And what of the final state of those who reject God's truth? "Therefore God gave them up in the lusts of their hearts to impurity, to the dishonoring of their bodies among themselves, *because they exchanged the truth about God for a lie* and worshiped and served the creature rather than the Creator, who is blessed forever!" (vv. 24, 25).

In man's search for truth, his greatest folly is to reject or discard Jesus Christ, the Creator and Redeemer, the Pioneer and Perfecter of faith, the One who is Truth itself.

Man is very foolish if he tries to engage in . . .

CHANGING THE RULES

The rules governing athletic events are established in advance. Players do not change them to suit themselves. Anyone who attempted to do so would rightfully he ridiculed.

The rules of life cannot be changed at will, either. God has established moral standards for the good of man, and man rejects them only to his own detriment.

History is filled with stories of men and of nations who have thought themselves above God. They have learned to their dismay that "God is not mocked, for whatever a man sows, that he will also reap" (Gal. 6:7, RSV).

The most recent attempt to cast aside God's moral absolutes is a movement advocated even by some *within* the Church—"situation ethics." In this view, man determines his behavior, not according to any precepts of God's revealed truth, but according to his own evaluation of the situation in which he finds himself at any given time.

Let us suppose for a moment this cavalier disregard for rules were applied to sports.

First, let's look at a baseball game. With a player on first and one out, the batter hits a sharp grounder to short. Cleanly

128

fielded—a throw to second and relay to first and the umpires signal both players "out."

But a rhubarb starts immediately. The batter claims he hit the ball so hard it should have been fumbled, while the runner thrown out at second yelled that he had made a perfect hook slide, even if the ball did get there ahead of him.

Despite their beefing, a perfect double play has been executed. No amount of arguing can change the umpires' decisions.

Now on to a football game. The fall classic between Yale and Harvard is under way. The ball is snapped from center and a draw play develops. The left end darts down the field, feints, and hooks back. At that moment the quarterback fires a perfect pass. But just as his teammate is about to catch the pass, an opposing player darts across his path, intercepts the ball, and with a brilliant burst of speed carries it over for a touchdown.

Immediately the quarterback protests to the umpire. He had had perfect protection and his pass had been straight as a die, he says. His intended receiver also protests, saying he had evaded his pursuers and, but for the interception, could well have scored for his team.

But of course it is ruled that there has been an interception and a touchdown, and that the six points counted for the opposing team.

What do the officials say?

The first-base umpire, dean of the National League arbiters, asks, "Wassa matter wid you guys? Ya gone nuts?"

And the referee asks "Who do you think you are? Do you think you can change the rules in the middle of the game?"

The determination to change the rules finds expression in the new morality, which puts situation ethics into practice.

There is the man whose wife has grown cold and who uses

this as an excuse to engage in extramarital relations. Both he and his partner in adultery excuse their action because it is "meaningful."

A boy and girl in college engage in premarital relations because they can see no reason for restraint and because there are others all around them who condone some fornication as an expression of "love."

A hard-working man yields to the temptation to gloss over certain items when reporting his income while at the same time he pads his expense account. "Everyone does it," he says, in trying to excuse himself.

Examples of rejection of the explicit teachings of the seventh and eighth commandments are legion. That God's laws are broken does not nullify them. When they are deliberately flouted in the name of "morality" or "ethics," it would seem that the acme of disobedience has been reached. Unless there is genuine repentance, surely there will come the judgment of a holy God.

The breakdown of morality that finds undergirding in situation ethics strikes at the very heart of personal and national life. When breaches of the moral law go uncondemned and are even approved and accepted, the foundations begin the crumble. The psalmist asks, "If the foundations are destroyed, what can the righteous do?" (Ps. 11:3).

Like a deadly gas, unrecognized at first, situation ethics is spreading across our land. Even some within the Church are welcoming and advancing it.

It is high time for Christians to awake and to recognize what is taking place.

One of America's most popular magazines recently published an article in which a prominent bishop sought to justify adultery under certain circumstances.

Also recently, a well-known religious journal carried an

article by a university professor of religion who advanced the case for the new morality:

. . . The free man is continually asking questions about what to do in respect to others: What is Susan's good? What is, or will be, wholeness for her? What can I do that will speed Susan's pilgrimage to the holy place of her own unique and complete identity? And from the free woman's side: What response will help John toward love for a woman who is wholly a woman? Even if he is willing impulsively to jeopardize his future, have I any right to encourage his doing so? What can I do or say that will create a relationship so fresh in all dimensions that no one of them is permitted to destroy the others? Set against such questions, the reductionist's formula, 'Yes, if married; no, if not,' seems merely silly ["Sex and the Single Standard," by Cyrus R. Pangborn, *The Christian Century*, May 17, 1967].

What foolishness! Situation ethics is a conception of morals in which there are no absolutes. Man must make his decisions on the basis of undefined "love," "fulfillment," "meaningfulness," and expediency.

This new approach to the temptations of life will have a devastating effect on all who succumb. That it is the subject of discussion on campuses and at young people's conferences adds to the danger. Without the restraining thought that God has established rules of moral behavior, and that man breaks those rules to his own harm, the whole fabric of society will be attacked by a form of spiritual cancer. The end of it all is inevitable judgment by the sovereign God—the Arbiter of time and eternity.

The Apostle Paul describes people who, "though they know God's decree that those who do such things deserve to die . . . not only do them but approve those who practice them" (Rom. 1:32).

And again Paul speaks: "For this is the will of God, your sanctification: that you abstain from immorality, . . . that no man transgress, and wrong his brother in this matter, because the Lord is an avenger in all these things, as we solemnly forewarned you. For God has not called us for uncleanness, but in holiness. Therefore whoever disregards this, disregards not man but God, who gives his Holy Spirit to you" (I Thess. 4:3, 6–8).

For men and for nations
the decision means . . .

TURMOIL OR PEACE

This is being written in a Western country, but it could be written anywhere, for the background is two large daily papers and three weekly news magazines that I have read in the last few hours.

What about the news and what it tells us of the world in which we live? On every hand unrest, disorder, crime, violence, poverty; everywhere tensions between man and man, race and race, nation and nation.

As I reflected upon this panorama of the day's events and one week's news, there came to mind the words of Jehovah to the Prophet Isaiah: "But the wicked are like the tossing sea; for it cannot rest, and its waters toss up mire and dirt. There is no peace, says my God, for the wicked" (Isa. 57:20, 21).

That the unregenerate world is definitely aware of the dangers of the existing turmoil is clearly shown by the fact that its leaders work so feverishly to reform and regulate society. There are those in the Church who see in this turmoil only evidence that "God is working out his purposes, often by revolutionary processes," while other Christians at-

133

tribute it all to Satan's destructive hand at work across the world and feel they should redouble their own efforts to witness to the saving and transforming power of Christ as man's only hope.

Can men reform the world? The answer is no!

Should God be blamed for the world's wickedness? The answer again is no! True, he does work out his holy purposes despite the sinfulness of men; and even causes the wrath of man to praise him; but that does not alter the fact that the evil about us is the work of Satan in the hearts and lives of men. The Apostle John makes plain the real distinction between Christians and the rest of the world: "We know that we are the children of God and that all the rest of the world around us is under man's power and control" (I John 19. The Living New Testament).

That the plight of the world is not hopeless is the reason for calling the Gospel the "Good News." God has given man the solution to his fearful predicament and has committed to the Church the task of telling this Good News.

Strange that we find ourselves living in a time when the Church itself is stressing reform above redemption and is often found teaming up with the world in an effort to work out "solutions" for the world's ills—without reference to Christ and his Cross.

Among the present-day theologians and teachers there are some, I feel, to whom God would say as he did through the Prophet Jeremiah, "Therefore, behold, I am against the prophets . . . who steal my words from one another. Behold, I am against the prophets . . . who use their tongues and say, 'Says the Lord.' Behold I am against those who prophesy lying dreams . . . and who tell them and lead my people astray by their lies and their recklessness, when I did not send them or charge them; so they do not profit this people at all . . ." (Jer. 23:30, 31).

Unquestionably one of the most serious of all problems is man's insensitivity to sin, his unwillingness to admit that the virus of evil is working all through his actions and reactions, his thoughts and desires, and that its ultimate end is death. This resisting and rejecting of God is common to the human race. Nothing less than the miracle of God's grace can enable us to see ourselves as we really are.

Not infrequently, perhaps, we Christians play a part in maintaining the general state of unrest by substituting activity for a quiet waiting on God. We forget the admonition: "For thus said the Lord God, the Holy One of Israel. 'In returning and rest you shall be saved; in quietness and in trust shall be your strength.' And you would not . . ." (Isa. 30:15). We forget that God is not dependent on human activity or organization. Useful as these may be, they are worth little unless subordinated to the leading and power of the Holy Spirit.

Living as we do in days of tremendous change, we as individual Christians and the Church as a whole *must* remember that God has laid a Foundation that never changes, established a Cross that is ageless and a hope that never fades. Let us think upon God's warning through Jeremiah: "Thus says the LORD: 'Stand by the roads and look, and ask for the ancient paths, where the good way is; and walk in it, and find rest for your souls.' But they said, 'We will not walk in it'" (Jer. 6:16).

In our efforts to reach young people through new "forms" or "methods," let us be sure that we do not try to change the message—that we are all sinners and that we need, and have, a Saviour!

Jerusalem was a city of turmoil in our Lord's day. It was under the domination of Rome, and the prevailing political cliques and religious hypocrisy, together with the ever present sickness and poverty, contributed to fear and unrest. Over that city our Lord wept, for he knew that they were rejecting their Redeemer: "O Jerusalem, Jerusalem, killing the prophets and stoning those who are sent to you! How often would I have gathered your children together as a hen gathers her brood under her wings, and you would not!" (Matt. 23:37).

We can well imagine our Lord's weeping in our own day over the world he created and came back to redeem, as he sees the conditions brought about by man's refusal to accede to God's way of redemption!

And how we Christians need to be reminded again and again of the peril of an empty profession. "Not every one who says to me, 'Lord, Lord,' shall enter the kingdom of Heaven, but he who does the will of my Father who is in heaven" (Matt. 7:21).

Profession, yes, but more is needed—there must be obedience in action!

In substituting philosophical presuppositions for revealed truth and rejecting the supernatural and the miraculous as did the Sadducees of old, the theological world and many within the Church are limiting the power of God and need to be reminded of our Lord's words: "You are wrong, because you know neither the scriptures nor the power of God" (Matt. 22:29).

The turmoil of the world today is the result of spiritual darkness. Man continues to choose darkness rather than light in preferring man—his thoughts, opinions and works—to God.

But out of the turmoil there can come rest; out of chaos, peace; out of darkness, light; and out of sickness of soul and spirit the marvelous health of redeeming love. That is the message of the Gospel, which is man's only hope now and for eternity.

The fact is, there are . . .

TWO KINGDOMS

Within the secular world order there are two kingdoms, concurrent in their present operation but totally different in nature and destiny.

The secular world is neutral. Here men work, eat, and play. Here the necessary activities of existence take place. None can escape this realm.

But spiritual forces work within the secular world and are not neutral. These form two totally diverse kingdoms. Satan captains one and administers it by his agents; the Son of God captains the other and administers it by his Spirit.

Until a man recognizes the difference between these two kingdoms and allows Christ to take charge of his life, there is only chaos, not peace, for him. Men and nations search futilely for the solution to their problems, not admitting that the only solution is Christ. The confusion of today's world is the confusion of persons who have never accepted the one solution of life (and death): Jesus Christ and his atoning and reconciling work on the Cross.

I recently read of a symposium involving students from three universities. The observations of these young people

137

were pitiful. The only convictions they shared were negative: they were against their parents, against the idea of moral or spiritual disciplines, and against the Church as such. They appeared ignorant of the meaning of life and displayed an agnostic irreverence for God and all things sacred.

An extreme illustration? Hardly. This new generation reflects the hypocrisy, sinfulness, and ignorance of parents who too often have sought material success or pleasure as the ultimate in life and given little thought to their own relationship to God. No man can be neutral to truth; he either accepts it or opposes it.

The kingdoms of God and Satan are not imaginary. God has revealed what they are and also their end. Man must face up to the situation and find out just where he stands.

A simple illustration may help to clarify our thinking. Recently I was on a plane about to depart from a large national airport. While the stewardess was checking the passengers' tickets, she discovered that one who was ticketed for Buffalo was seated there on that plane—headed for Atlanta. No amount of arguing could have changed the fact that the passenger intended to go one way but was really going in the opposite direction.

Every person in this world is a member of Satan's kingdom until he becomes a member of God's kingdom. Philosophical arguments cannot change the situation. But we can thank God who has shown the difference between them and made clear the fact that anyone willing to change need not remain in the domain of Satan.

Satan's kingdom is counterfeit. It is part of the dying world order. He incites his victims to follow the dictates of natural desire. He knows that the wages paid by sin is death—spiritual death and eternal separation from God. That is Satan's desire for every man.

God's kingdom, which is spiritual, consists of those who have changed their citizenship through faith in Jesus Christ. Jesus said, "You must be born again," and made it clear that rebirth is a work of God by which one is translated from the kingdom of death to the kingdom of life.

The two kingdoms will always differ. Satan's kingdom is one of spiritual darkness, frustration, and hopelessness. God's kingdom is one of light, joy, and hope. Although its citizens are not spared the vicissitudes of life, they have grace to rise above them.

The Apostle Paul speaks of the grace and peace that come from God the Father and the Lord Jesus Christ, "who gave himself for our sins to deliver us from the present evil age . . ." (Gal. 1:4, RSV).

Deliverance from Satan's kingdom is made *by* Christ, and life in God's eternal kingdom is lived *with* Christ. Without his atoning death and resurrection, there could be no change. Through them, the way to freedom is open to "whosoever will."

Men are members of either one kingdom or the other and are destined to go either to heaven or to hell. Jesus used these terms, not to frighten people, but to impress upon them the consequences of this choice. Paul states it in these terms: "For many . . . live as enemies of the cross of Christ. Their end is destruction, their God is the belly, and they glory in their shame, with minds set on earthly things. But our commonwealth is in heaven, and from it we await a Saviour, the Lord Jesus Christ, who will change our lowly body to be like his glorious body, by the power which enables him even to subject all things to himself" (Phil. 3:18–21).

Indication of the diametrically opposed kingdoms is seen in life's contrasts: in the opposites of good and evil, of right and wrong, of hope and hopelessness, of peace and turmoil, of joy and sorrow, of meaning and meaninglessness in life.

Transition from one kingdom to the other is at the very

heart of the gospel message. This change is supernatural, a work of the Spirit of God. The rule of the one who is the epitome of evil and hatred is exchanged for that of the One who acts righteously and in love, and whose concern is for our eternal welfare.

One's warfare does not end when he accepts Christ. In fact, up to that time things are often ominously quiet; but the moment one receives Christ as Saviour and Lord, the true war begins. This is war with the "unseen" power that controls this dark world, and spiritual agents from the very headquarters of evil" (Eph. 6:12, Phillips). But the protective armor and the sword of the Spirit are given, and victory is assured.

To fail to recognize the existence of spiritual warfare, of the two kingdoms, is to play directly into the hands of the enemy. But to recognize the situation for what it really is and take a stand on the side of God and his kingdom assures one of ultimate victory.

We live in a supposedly enlightened age; but until we recognize the role of Satan, until we make a decision for Christ and accept God's plan and will for us, we are living in spiritual darkness.

The evidence is everywhere for us to see. The reasons are clearly stated in the Word of God. The doctrines of man's need and hope are all part of the gospel message. If we continue in ignorance or reject God's plan for deliverance, we have no one to blame but ourselves.

Man's conflict began when he disobeyed God. The final outcome of the conflict was determined at Calvary.

Of which kingdom are you a citizen?

Keep the communication lines open,
don't be guilty of . . .

A WILLFUL BLACK-OUT

A man is lost in the desert, desperately in need of water, food, and a way out. He has with him a two-way radio in perfect condition. By it he could learn where to find water, food, and a compass to lead him home.

But the man does not use the radio! He pays no attention to the clearly printed instructions on how to turn it on, tune in, and maintain a two-way conversation. The batteries are fully charged, and at the other end there is an operator always on the job; but because of his utter foolishness, the wanderer remains lost, parched, and famished.

Christians must acknowledge that they are "strangers and exiles on the earth" (Heb. 11:13, RSV) and constantly in need of God's help and guidance. Strange indeed how often we are confused, lost, spiritually thirsty and hungry, despite the promise: "If you abide in me, and my words abide in you, ask whatever you will, and it shall be done for you" (John 15:7).

We are told that our Lord "marveled" at the unbelief of those who should have heard and obeyed him. Isaiah tells us of God's reaction to man's blind perversity—he "wondered that there was no one to intervene" (Isa. 59:16b).

Certainly one of the strangest things in all the world today is the Christian's failure to avail himself of the privilege and power of prayer! True, the prayerless Christian is not "lost" in terms of eternity. But all of us experience daily need for spiritual blessings that come only through communion with God.

Prayer is not using God for our own ends. It is not, "O God, do this or that for me." Prayer is something infinitely higher and more precious than that. Prayer is two-way communion with God, praising his name, glorifying him for what he is and what he has done. Prayer is bringing our worship to him and seeking his glory in all circumstances of life.

Some may say, "How pietistic." "How far removed from our world and its problems." "How impractical in the face of the demands of the twentieth century." "How utterly removed from the real problems that trouble men in this space age."

But wait a minute. Does any problem ever take God by surprise? Is any issue of today too big for him to solve? Has he made promises to his children that he is now unable to fulfill? Has the space age left God behind? Are we living in a maze of problems from which even the Creator and Sovereign God of the universe cannot extract us?

Perhaps the best way to answer these questions is to take God at his word and give him a chance to make it good.

Jesus has made us a tremendous promise: "Ask whatever you will, and it shall be done for you." Are there conditions? Of course; otherwise prayer would prove to be our destruction, not a blessing. But there are only two conditions, our abiding in him and having his words abide in us. Abiding in Christ means resting in him, obeying him, having our old lives replaced by lives filled with his presence.

The Apostle Paul expresses this thought of "abiding" in Christ in words all of us can understand: "I have been crucified with Christ; it is no longer I who live, but Christ who lives in me; and the life I now live in the flesh I live by faith in the Son of God, who loved me and gave himself for me" (Gal. 2:20).

Is this something too high for us? Did Paul have an experience with Christ denied to others? Can we have our old natures crucified with Christ and live by a new and supernatural power—the power of the crucified and risen Christ? Yes, we can. And in this experience we become new creatures, spiritually born again, with a new line of communication with the living God opened to us.

How can his words "abide in" us? Jesus simply meant that his teachings, his truth, his revealed will, must be kept fresh in our memories and be the basic motivation in our lives. Christianity is not a dreamy, mystical religion. It is a faith to be believed and a life to be lived according to God's revealed truth.

In the time of Ezra there came upon the people a mighty conviction of sin. They had neglected the Word of God and disobeyed its teachings, and we are told that they "trembled" when they realized what they had done. It would be well for us to tremble also at the way we have neglected, ignored, and disobeyed the revelation God has given us in his written Word.

Every Christian can fulfill these two conditions, abiding in Christ and having his words abide in us. Then why live as beggars in the midst of plenty? Why neglect the privilege and opportunity God has opened to each of his children? Some day, in heaven, we will look back in amazement at our present failure to use prayer as we should.

For Christians the horizon of prayer is unlimited—not

simply for us to get things from God but for his will to be done both in our individual lives and in the circumstances of life.

We do not pray alone. Paul tells us that Christ "is at the right hand of God" and "intercedes for us." And "likewise the Spirit helps us in our weakness; for we know not how to pray as we ought, but the Spirit himself intercedes for us with sighs too deep for words" (Rom. 8:34 and 26).

Prayer is intensely practical. There is not an hour of the day that we don't need the wisdom, strength, and guidance God alone can supply. There is not a problem, a concern for others, a sorrow, or a joy that should not be shared with the One who has the answer, the hope, the balm.

Because prayer is such a power for good, Satan hates it. He and all the real though unseen demons of hell conspire to keep us from communing with God.

First of all Satan would interpose between us and God sin that we have not confessed and repented of. "If I had cherished iniquity in my heart, the Lord would not have listened" (Ps. 66:18). Satan tries to make us doubt the love and power of God and to make our thoughts and desires selfish. Pride, one of his most frequently used weapons, is often our downfall. Or it may be an unloving heart or an unwillingness to forgive that stands between us and God. We must not forget that as Christ has forgiven us to the limit, so we must forgive others to the limit.

Let me conclude on a note of personal witness. I *know* that God hears and answers prayer—sometimes before we pray—in the way that is best, and for his own glory.

There are times when the answer seems to take a long time coming, but God knows best. And there are times when the answer is so miraculous that one's heart nearly bursts with wonder and praise.

Prayer is more powerful than nuclear fission, and as wonderful as creation itself. Little wonder that Paul tells us to "pray without ceasing"—that is, to keep communications open all the time.

Know your Bible or you will be guilty of . . .

ERROR THROUGH IGNORANCE

The greatest protection from error is knowing the truth. "What you do not know will not hurt you"—this does not apply to the Christian and his Bible. Much more applicable is Alexander Pope's dictum, "A little learning is a dangerous thing; drink deep, or taste not the Pierian spring." Error stems from ignorance and superficial knowledge.

In the Scriptures we find Truth—a revelation of things man can never discover from any other source. How great, then, is the ignorance of those who do not know or willfully neglect the Scriptures, who capriciously question them or reject them outright.

The Sadducees, who denied the concept of the supernatural and miraculous, of course rejected out of hand the reality of the resurrection. On one occasion a group of them came to Jesus with an absurd hypothetical story about seven brothers who had died, one after the other, and who in accordance with the law of Moses had in succession married the older brother's wife. Now the Sadducees asked triumphantly, "In the resurrection whose wife will she be? For the seven had her as wife" (Mark 12:23).

146

Our Lord's reply must have been devastating for them, and it also speaks volumes to us today: "Is not this why you are wrong, that you know neither the scriptures nor the power of God?"

The Sadducees were involved in a theological error about the resurrection because they were ignorant of the Scriptures. And being ignorant of the Scriptures, they were also ignorant of God's power.

Within the Church today, even in many theological seminaries, the prevalent ignorance of the Bible is appalling. The modern-day Sadducees consider the supernatural and miraculous suspect. Many persons look upon the Scriptures as a more or less human document, and therefore discount their worth. In so doing they remain ignorant of the truth and the power of the living God.

Even a casual conversation with the average Christian will reveal ignorance of the Word. It may be that the pressures of daily living have crowded the Bible out of its rightful place, or that some casual seed of criticism has grown into a tree of unbelief. Whatever the cause, the result is disastrous, for out of ignorance comes error, not only such deviations as may be found in the cults that thrive on every hand, but devastating errors having to do with God and man, good and evil, sin and judgment, time and eternity, heaven and hell, and above all else, Christ and redemption.

Ignorance of the Word of God leads to futility and frustration and accounts for the world's tumult as well as for disordered individual lives. It leads up every blind alley of the human mind and to the "wisdom of this world," which is folly with God.

We are told that man has come of age, and that he is now capable of living without God. How far will such foolishness go? If man sows the seeds of rejection of God, he will surely reap the harvest of rejection *by* God.

What, then, should we do?

This is a plea that men replace their ignorance of the Bible by a knowledge that not only will stand the test against error but also will bring into true perspective the power of God in the redeeming work of his Son, in the indwelling presence of his Spirit, and in the written Word. When this is done, God leads the willing and obedient heart into all truth, and in that truth there is a freedom otherwise unknown.

To give the Bible its rightful place is to recognize that daily Bible study is as important for spiritual growth as is food for the physical body.

It also means that the Bible is allowed to speak for itself. While it is true that some people take "proof texts" out of context, thereby coming up with some invalid conclusions, nevertheless those saturated with the Word attain a perspective that enables them to rise to any situation and apply to it the clear teachings of this divine revelation.

In Josiah's time reformation came when the Law of Moses was discovered and reapplied to personal and national life.

The false doctrines of Jesus' day were the result of ignorance of the Scriptures together with the practice of "teaching for doctrines the precepts of men" (Matt. 15:9).

During the Dark Ages the Bible was kept from the people with tragic results, but with the Protestant Reformation there came a release of the Word through the translation and circulation of the Bible. This ushered in a new era of personal and corporate Christianity.

Today, the most flourishing churches are those that honor the Bible. And the nations with the greatest degree of moral light have been those where the Word was best known. Where the Bible is known and obeyed, we find also more true personal religion. The godliest families are found to give the Scriptures top priority, and those who live closest to God are the ones who make the Bible their own infallible rule of faith and practice.

To live thus is bound to arouse some opposition—many times fierce opposition. Satan's sneering question, "Yea, hath God said?" (Gen. 3:1), is asked in every generation—the difference today being that the Bible is most vigorously attacked from *within* the Church.

Let not sneering criticism, outright opposition, or any other device of Satan deter you from reading, studying, believing, and obeying God's Word! It is truly the "Sword of the Spirit," and Satan has never been able to stand against it.

Far from being "obsolete" or "irrelevant" to today's world, the Bible is the most up-to-date and relevant book in all the world. In Proverbs alone young people can find answers for all the problems that confront them. The Psalms put into words the holiest and highest aspirations of the human heart, as well as words of worship and praise that lift the soul to the heights of spiritual expression.

Make Bible study as much a part of your daily program as your meals, work, and exercise. Study it book by book, or choose a theme and follow it through. Do not fail to read the Scriptures through to catch the continuity of God's revelation to man. Take a fine red pencil and underline passages that speak a special message to your heart. This will be a help at the time and a blessing in subsequent studies.

For the faithful student of the Word there are unending surprises as passages suddenly take on new meaning, often speaking to a specific need of that time. Believe what you read and obey God's leading. Like the psalmist, pray to see God's truth: "Let my cry come before thee, O LORD; give me understanding according to thy word" (Ps. 119:169).

The Bible is . . .

THE UNIQUE BOOK

There is a famous bookstore in Washington, D.C., that I visit frequently. Almost daily new books are on display. Many have eye-catching jackets, and often the publisher's blurb gives the impression that anyone who does not read this book will suffer from ignorance about earth-changing personalities or events.

Unquestionably many of these books are interesting, instructive, or thought-provoking. Others portray moral filth in attractive and sophisticated ways. But one ventures the conviction that in all of the tens of thousands of books available—good or bad—there is not one single volume that is of *eternal* significance to its readers—except the Bible.

Despite all our advantages, we as a people suffer from the greatest of all deficiencies—spiritual starvation—because of our ignorance of the Bible. Let's think for a moment about this Book that is so available and so neglected.

The Bible is certainly the *only* book in all the world that comes with the seal of divine authority resting upon it. In its pages God speaks to man so that he sees himself as God sees him, and sees time and eternity in their proper perspective.

Every spiritual awakening has been accompanied by a turning to the Scriptures for instruction and light on the daily path.

The Bible is a book of many facets, and the ways in which its teachings can be brought to bear upon our lives are limitless. As a physician, I often see medical analogies in its pages and have often noted that in a very real sense the Scriptures are like a spiritual X-ray. We read in Hebrews 4:13: "Before him no creature is hidden, but all are open and laid bare to the eyes of him with whom we have to do."

Some years ago a woman walked into my office, limping and complaining of increasing pain in her foot. One look through the fluoroscope showed me that a sewing needle was imbedded in the sole of her foot. Removal was easy, and before long the pain was relieved and the patient cured.

The world—even some church members—goes limping along with personal and social problems unresolved because God has not been permitted to speak through his Word, diagnose the disease and offer a cure. Many true Christians are miserable, at outs with themselves and others. They long for the peace and joy that should be theirs in Christ but never permit the searching light of God's truth to enter their hearts and reveal the sickness there.

The Bible may also be likened to a mirror in which we see ourselves as we really are. Many are unwilling to look into it because of their fear of what they may see.

Years ago a Confucian scholar was brought into our missionary hospital with a broken hip. During the weeks he was with us he was given a Bible to read, and the night before he was dismissed he gave a feast for the staff. With typical Oriental courtesy he expressed appreciation for the care given him. Then he continued, "When I came to this hospital I thought I was a good man. I had tried to lead an honorable life and had done a great deal for the poor. But after reading the Bible, I saw myself as I really was, and I saw too that

God had made provision for a sinner like me in the death of his Son on the Cross. I am leaving this hospital believing in Christ as my Saviour."

We also find that the Bible is at times truly like a sword—"the Sword of the Spirit." As such it pierces the respectability that we put on as a cloak. It goes to the heart of the matter to discern "the thoughts and intentions of the heart." Only this morning I was reading a portion of Scripture that exposed a secret sin in my heart.

At the core of the Holy Scriptures is found Jesus Christ, the Son of God. To him both the Old and the New Testament bear witness. Paul indicated this in writing to his spiritual son Timothy: "But as for you, continue in what you have learned and have firmly believed, knowing from whom you learned it and how from childhood you have been acquainted with the sacred writings which are able to instruct you for salvation through faith in Christ Jesus" (II Tim. 3:15).

We tend to look for Christ only in the New Testament, but the risen Christ himself said to his disciples, "These are my words which I spoke to you, while I was still with you, that everything written about me in the law of Moses and the prophets and the psalms must be fulfilled" (Luke 24:44).

To divest Christ of his supernatural and miraculous nature, work, and power is to talk of a Christ who never existed. To accept him as he is means a transformed life and destiny.

The Apostle Paul makes a bold assertion (and experience shows the folly of denying its truth) that all Scripture is inspired by God. Because of this it is profitable:

First, for *teaching*. The world searches for knowledge, but the Bible gives true wisdom. Lacking the insights afforded by this wisdom, man gropes in the darkness of human speculation. Secular education leads to knowledge about many things, but true wisdom and understanding are found only in the divine revelation. It is hard for the academic world to accept the fact that "the fear of the Lord is the beginning of wisdom." Far easier to deny or ignore him!

The Bible is also profitable for *reproof*. The world is suffering from sin, and sin must be reproved. Men are going in the wrong direction and need to be told of that fact. Permissiveness in matters of eternal import is folly. The Bible calls sin sin.

In addition to teaching and reproving, the Bible has power to *correct*. It shows the difference between good and evil, between right and wrong. As glasses correct vision or a cast corrects a bone weakness, the Bible speaks clearly and frankly about what God requires of man and tells of his provision to that end.

The Bible *trains* in righteousness, makes the Christian *complete*, and *equips* him for every good work.

Finally, the Bible is the only book that authoritatively speaks of the past, the present, and the future. In its pages are to be found the answers to the problems and pressures of life.

Little wonder that Satan hates God's Word! From the beginning he has asked insinuatingly, "Did God say?" He fears the Bible because it *is* the "Sword of the Spirit" against which he cannot stand. His greatest victory today is among those in whom he has planted a seed of doubt, by frank denial or by insinuation, in classrooms, in books, and in the pulpit itself.

God's words through Jeremiah speak to us today: "The wise men shall be put to shame, they shall be dismayed and taken: lo, they have rejected the word of the LORD, and what wisdom is in them?" (Jer. 8:9).

But to the believer he also speaks: "For ever, O LORD, thy word is firmly fixed in the heavens." "The unfolding of thy

words gives light; it imparts understanding to the simple"
(Ps. 119:89, 130).

May our response be: "I rejoice at thy word like one who
finds great spoil" (Ps. 119:162).

It's worth trying, because it works!

It is also . . .

THE LIVING BOOK

Imagine an oceangoing liner without anchor, compass, or rudder. Wrecking and loss would be inevitable. And all round us, inside and outside the Church, there are millions of people in an analogous spiritual condition.

Day after day countless Christians start out without any conscious anchor of the soul, without a compass by which their lives can be properly oriented, and without the rudder of God's guidance to enable them to steer a straight course through the confusing situations of life.

This happens to all who do not know and use the Bible, the written Word of God; for it is the Bible that is an anchor in the midst of shifting opinions, a compass that orients us to God's eternal verities, and a rudder that turns man toward God's mercy. Above all else, the Bible tells us of Christ and how we may obtain salvation through faith in him.

The world is full of changing opinions. The speculations of men are as numerous and as varied as men themselves. On every hand voices clamor to be heard; some are foolish, some wise, but all are subject to change with the passing of time. In the midst of this situation, the Bible stands as an unending source of wisdom. In it are found the answers so many seek but rarely find; for the wisdom of this Book is divine, a revelation of truth man can never uncover from any other source.

Since this is so (and it can be put to the test by anyone), what should our attitude toward the Bible be?

I speak from a long and soul-satisfying experience. I know the aridness and frustration of days lived without the comfort and guidance of the Scriptures. I also know the joy that comes when things and events fall into a clear pattern because the Captain and His Word have been consulted at the beginning of the day, and because divine wisdom has been given precedence over human opinions.

The daily reading of the Bible and the appropriation of the things it has to offer are of such great importance, and the end result so soul-satisfying, that it cannot be overemphasized.

We live in a secularized and materialistic world. Only in the Bible and through the grace of the Holy Spirit can we come to know and appreciate spiritual values, and compare them with the values of a world alienated from God. The Bible points us in the right direction in the midst of conflicting claims. It shows us *the* way, even when the sun is obscured by clouds of adversity and the fogs of doubt surround us. Like a brilliant light, the Bible shows the path of God in the midst of other paths that beckon to ultimate disaster.

In our time moral values are considered to be relative, not absolute; right and wrong are said to be determined by the situation, not by a moral code. It is clear that Satan has undermined the morality that is a basic part of the Judeo-Christian tradition.

How can young people—or any of us—live lives of purity

when all around there are enticements to violate the moral standards on which our society has been built?

In the Book of Proverbs, young people can find the answers to their problems today. Bookstores stock hundreds of books containing advice to young people, but the clear teachings of this marvelously modern Old Testament book have never been surpassed or superseded.

Who does not have problems? There is hardly a day when we are not confronted with them in one way or another; but the man whose mind is steeped in the Word of God can find basic answers to life's problems. The answer may be a warning against the personal sins that lie at the root of the problems; or it may be a word giving the solution as a light flashing in the dark.

In our time knowledge has multiplied astonishingly, and it probably will continue to multiply far beyond the capability of man to make use of it. But over and beyond all that may be learned about the world there is the fact of God's transcendent wisdom offered to man in the Bible, without which he continues to be an earthbound creature. This wisdom can bring peace of heart and serenity of mind because it is fixed on the One who is Truth itself.

No one would deny that our world is full of staggering uncertainties. Many suffer from the constant tensions caused by an unknown future. Wars and rumors of wars are only a part of a world where political, social, and economic ferments point to possible disaster.

Yet he who has his faith firmly rooted in the Word of God sees beyond these uncertainties. He has an anchor that reaches far beyond what is visible, and he *knows* that no turn of events can separate him from the love of God. He *knows* that God is sovereign, and that all that occurs is permitted by him. He *knows* that all things in his own life are working out for his good, because he loves God.

In the Bible, and nowhere else, a man can find an unfailing frame of reference. On every hand the lives of men are being shipwrecked because they have nothing to hold them steady amid the temptations to which they are subjected. This is tragically true within the Church when men accept a low view of the inspiration and authority of the Word.

On the personal level, the Bible is an unending source of comfort and hope. Who has not had his spirit lifted by the affirmations and promises in the Word? Who has not had his soul buoyed up by the sure hope that comes from this source? Whose heart has not found expressed in the Psalms the words of praise and thanksgiving he feels to the God of love who has dealt so wondrously with his erring children? As in no other literature, the heart's deepest feelings find articulation in the Psalms.

Like a man dying of dehydration when a gushing spring is near at hand, or one starving when a feast is within his reach, so men and women are perishing because they do not make daily use of the Book that is found in almost every household.

With the reading of the Word there comes spiritual enlightenment, growing confidence, and adjusted perspectives. There is no substitute for the Bible. Books about the Bible have an important place; but they are at best the words of men, and too often they are tainted by unbelief.

The Bible is a *living* book, more relevant than tomorrow morning's newspaper. It is not, of course, to be worshiped; we worship the Christ it reveals. It is not a fetish but a living revelation from the living God.

I challenge all who read this to test these claims for themselves.

Let me speak . . .

FOR A FRIEND

I speak for a friend downgraded by some, laughed at by others. I speak for a friend, the victim of unjust criticism, picked apart here and rejected there. I speak for a friend accused of being irrelevant for our times and even of being a fraud. But I speak for a friend greatly loved and proved true and trustworthy over the years, by me and by countless others.

I speak for the Bible, the written Word of God. Despite the often heard assertion, "The Bible needs no defense," surely its friends should not remain silent in the face of irresponsible criticism that may lead others to ignore, neglect, or reject it.

The integrity and authority of this friend, the Holy Scriptures, are at stake. Little by little men are whittling away at both, and in so doing they are striking at the Son of God, revealed in the Word.

We who accept the complete trustworthiness of the Bible can do so on the basis of sound reasoning. It is inconceivable that God would have given a revelation, part of which was subject to question.

Above all else, we believe the Bible because of the Christ revealed therein. The Lord must become experientially real to all Christians, but *only in the Bible* do we find who he is, what he did, and why he did it, and our overwhelming need of him as Saviour and Lord. Eliminate the biblical record and only vain speculation is left. Accept that record and there is revealed—in all his beauty and power—Jesus Christ, the Son of the Living God.

I speak a word for the Bible because there, in the clearest possible perspective, one can see God at work in his creation and history. One sees, etched in words of fire, his own need and God's provision for that need. Without the Word there would be no explanation for man's existence, his predicament, and his hope. In the light of the Word, this world and the next fall into their proper relationships.

I speak for the Word because our Lord himself did not hesitate to make use of the Old Testament Scriptures, referring to them as accurate and authoritative. Were it not for our Lord's use of the Scriptures, we would be ignorant of the meaning of many passages that refer to him. His simple statement, ". . . that everything written about me in the law of Moses and the prophets and the psalms must be fulfilled" (Luke 24:44, RSV), should impel us to search the Scriptures, which, our Lord said, "speak of me."

I speak for the written Word because the apostles in their writings refer again and again to the Old Testament Scriptures in such a way as to affirm their complete truthfulness and authority.

Those who today inveigh against "proof texts" would do well to notice how frequently Jesus, and later his disciples, used such texts. Furthermore, it is noteworthy that these critics of "proof texts" do not hesitate to resort to the same authoritative source when to do so suits their purpose.

I speak a word for the Holy Scriptures because of the claims they make for themselves. They claim the inspiration of the Holy Spirit for what was written. Again and again we read the words of the prophets, "Thus saith the Lord," and we sense that only God could so speak.

When we read the Apostle Paul's bold statement, "All scripture is inspired by God . . ." (II Tim. 3:16), or the Apostle Peter's words, ". . . no prophecy of scripture is a matter of one's own interpretation, because no prophecy ever came by the impulse of man, but men moved by the Holy Spirit spoke from God" (II Pet. 1:20, 21), we are led to believe and to thank God that this was so.

There are those who sneeringly say that some of us worship the Bible, that we are "bibliolaters." How foolish men can get! I know of no person who worships the Bible, but I know of many who worship the Christ revealed therein. A surgeon does not worship his scalpel; but he trusts it. So those who have approached the Word of God with faith, who through the Holy Spirit have come to understand it and by the help of God have tried to obey it, are convinced that the Bible is what it claims to be, the written Word of God.

I speak a word for the Bible because inherent in it is a power present and possible only where the Holy Spirit reigns. The Apostle Paul described the written Word as the "sword of the Spirit." Our Lord used three thrusts of this sword to defeat Satan in the wilderness. It has been used again and again by believers to stand firm in the face of the devil's attacks.

Furthermore, preaching that is saturated with the Word of God, that is based on and confirmed by this divine revelation, touches hearts with the awareness of sin and transforms indifference into conviction and action. "Thus saith the Lord" still has its ancient power; God's Word is "living and active, sharper than any two-edged sword, piercing to the division of soul and spirit, of joints and marrow, and discerning the thoughts and intentions of the heart" (Heb. 4:12).

I speak a word for the Holy Scriptures because of what they mean to me. They speak to my heart and go down to the innermost parts of my soul. Through them I hear someone speaking, and there is no question who it is. As the Bible speaks I accept it by faith; and having done this, I find that the way to understanding is opened. Not that I understand all. No one would be so foolish as to deny that there are depths of mystery whose edges we barely touch. It could not be otherwise; in the world the divine revelation is seen only dimly. We contemplate the universe with awe and reverence; how much more should we worship and praise the God of that universe for who he is and what he has done for us.

I also speak for the written Word of God because it expresses my soul's deepest feelings and aspirations. David, who our Lord says was "inspired by the Spirit" (Matt. 22:43), not only gives us in the Psalms revealed truth and prophecy but also lifts our souls to heights of adoration and praise of God without which we would be poor indeed.

Finally, I speak a word for the Scriptures because I have tested God's marvelous promises and found them true. He promises to guide, and when we turn to him he does just that. He promises to give wisdom, and when we admit our own insufficiency and lean on him he does not fail. He offers to help us in every contingency of life, and he makes good his offer. When sorrow comes he gives solace. With temptations he offers the way of escape. When his Kingdom is given precedence, the necessities of life are assured.

Yes, I am speaking for a friend; one ignored, maligned, neglected, down-graded, and often openly denied. I speak because in my heart I know the Scriptures are to be trusted, and by experience I know they are true. This is a love affair that has grown with the years. Where once a verse or a short passage made up the day's reading, now there is *joy* in extended study. As in praying, so in reading the Holy Scriptures one meets God face to face. He brings rest for the soul today and hope for the future, in the person and work of his Son.

Comparisons can be invidious, but
when you come to the
Bible think of these and don't be . . .

UTTERLY FOOLISH!

A ship sets sail across the ocean. It carries neither pilot nor compass. What would you say of the owner and of the captain of the ship?

A plane starts a flight across the North Pole. There is no navigator on board and no way to chart the course. One would rightly question the sanity of the crew.

A man starts to drive across the United States. He does not provide himself with road maps, nor does he ask anyone what route to take. He would almost certainly take the wrong roads.

A man becomes acutely ill. Neither he nor his family will call the doctor, nor will he take any medicine. What would one think of such people?

A soldier goes into battle. He takes with him neither gun, nor ammunition, nor any kind of weapon with which to attack

164

the enemy or defend himself. He would be a very foolish soldier.

A student enters a classroom to get ready for an examination. He puts cotton in his ears so that he cannot hear the teacher and closes his eyes so that he cannot read his books. He would well deserve a "dunce cap."

A physician goes into surgery to operate on a patient but refuses to use the necessary instruments. Would you want him to operate on you?

A lawyer goes into court to defend a client, but he does not know the points of law involved, nor can he argue the case. What would people think of such an advocate?

The owner of a large store has no inventory of his stock, nor does he know the cost of the items on the shelves. Failure in business would inevitably be his lot.

A motorist driving at night refuses to turn on the lights. Can you figure him out?

A carpenter attempts to build a house, but he will not use a square, saw, hammer, or plane. What kind of a house can he build?

A house is wired for electricity, and all the fixtures are in place. But the owner refuses to turn the switches for either light or power. Only one deprived of his senses would act so foolishly.

A man is walking down a dark road at night. He does not

know the road. He has in his hand a flashlight that he will not use. What would you think of such a person?

A bridge is washed out, and the highway patrol sets up warning lights and a barricade. A motorist refuses to stop and crashes to his death. Who was to blame?

One's natural reaction to these imagined absurdities is: Only a fool would act like that.

The world is full of fools, men and women who are ignoring the only Book that contains the chart and compass for living and for dying.

The Bible above all else tells us of the Pilot of our souls, the Redeemer from sin, the One who is the Way, the Truth and the Life, the only Saviour of mankind.

This Book gives us a map of the past, the present, and the future. By it alone can history be understood, and today's news explained, and tomorrow's events evaluated.

Much is being said today about man's moral and ethical responsibilities, but unless these are based on the teachings of God's written Word they are futile. It is because men have left (or never known) true Christian ethics that they now talk of "situation ethics"—do what you consider right under the circumstances in which you find yourself.

We are engaged in a daily battle with Satan. Only in the Bible do we learn of his methods, his plans, his ultimate destiny, and the way to gain victory over him.

Books on psychology and on human personality and behavior are legion. But only in the Bible do we learn the underlying issues of life and how to meet them.

In our day, moral and spiritual values have lost their meaning for many. Our generation has largely cut loose from its moorings and does not know where it is going or what to do. The concepts that are based on the rightness or wrongness of behavior are largely lost and cannot be replaced by mere human philosophy.

In the Bible we find a clear statement of the values that are based on God's holiness. There we find an anchor for the soul in terms the Spirit interprets. There we are confronted with the situations of everyday life and told how God would have his children act.

The Psalmist, extolling the blessings of God's Word available to all who will believe and obey, says: "Thy word is a lamp to my feet and a light to my path" (Ps. 119:105). Has there ever been a time when men needed light for daily living more than today? To ignore this divinely given light is a crime against our own souls. In this same psalm we read a prayer that should be voiced constantly by every Christian: "Keep steady my steps according to thy promise, and let no iniquity get dominion over me" (v. 133).

The foolish persons described at the beginning of this article should make each of us consider his own attitude toward the Bible. If we are neglecting it, we are doing so to our eternal loss and our daily confusion. For without God and the revelation he has given us of *how* we should live and what we should do, we continue as blind fools, willfully rejecting the light. We may be advanced in every form of knowledge. We may master multitudinous scientific facts and be aware of the many ramifications of human wisdom. But only by the Bible do we find the searchlight of the Spirit revealing our own hearts and at the same time showing us the way in which we should walk.

In the Bible we learn how to be saved. Paul told Timothy that it was the Holy Scriptures that are able to make us wise unto salvation, for there we find the Christ. For each of us there must be a personal *experience* with the living Christ, but with that experience there must be an *understanding* of who he is, of his Person and Work. Others may expand and interpret the meaning to us; but in the Bible, by the Spirit, we meet him face to face.

We should be trained soldiers, knowing how to use the Sword of the Spirit; enlightened guides, able to teach others the unsearchable riches of the books. We should be wise with a wisdom from above, thereby distinguishing between the true and the false.

The satanic question, "Yea, hath God said?," is still heard today. Those who are wise will let the Bible speak for itself.

Those who reject or neglect the Word are foolish indeed, for "the unfolding of thy words gives light; it imparts understanding to the simple" (Ps. 119: 130).

Stop and consider the difference between . . .

REVELATION AND REASON

Is Christianity reasonable? Only if human reason is properly related to faith.

I am quite aware that this statement may appear "unreasonable," but I believe it lies at the very heart of the predicament of unregenerate man.

The "preaching of the Cross" is nothing but foolishness to those who do not believe. The offense of the Cross is its revealing both man's utter helplessness and God's way of redeeming him—through a Person and an act far transcending human experience and wisdom.

Revelation is solely from and by God. Reason is a human faculty given to man by God. By divine fiat man was granted the power to say yes and to say no. And he is held accountable for his choice. Wrong choices based on faulty reasoning carry grave penalties.

Years ago Pollock remarked that, for many persons, "reasoning" is the great obstacle to conversion. This is perhaps even more true of people today. Basic theological problems emerge when reason is given priority over faith.

One extreme is the "God is dead" philosophy, where human reason has become sterile rationalism: man becomes his own god, and God is ruled out of existence.

The Apostle Paul, preaching in Lystra against the idolatry of that city, told of God's dealings with mankind from the time of the creation and said, "Yet he did not leave himself without witness" (Acts 14:17a, RSV). This witness is the revelation he has given us of himself and his truth.

The revelation of God in creation is continuing and universal. "The heavens are telling the glory of God; and the firmament proclaims his handiwork. Day to day pours forth speech, and night to night declares knowledge. There is no speech, nor are there words; their voice is not heard; yet their voice goes out through all the earth, and their words to the end of the world" (Ps. 19:1–4a).

The Apostle Paul speaks of the revelation of God's works of creation as entailing man's responsibility: "Ever since the creation of the world his invisible nature, namely, his eternal power and deity, has been clearly perceived in the things that have been made. So they are without excuse" (Rom. 1:20). Because revelation is the foundation of Christianity, *faith must be given precedence over mere human reason*. In view of the implications of revelation, there obviously is much that man cannot understand this side of eternity. If it were otherwise, revelation would be unnecessary. There is much that must be accepted by faith, which often transcends human reason.

God also reveals himself and his truth in his acts of providence and control—in our personal lives, in current events, in history. This revelation must be believed even though we do not always understand God's ways. By faith we see the operation of the divine and omnipotent hand that moves in such a mysterious way through our own lives and through history. The Apostle Paul was led to exclaim, "O the depth of the riches and wisdom and knowledge of God! How unsearchable are his judgments and how inscrutable his ways!" (Rom. 11: 33). This was an affirmation of faith, not of human reason.

The abundance of God's revelation to man is also seen in his Written Word. How limited our knowledge and understanding would be without the Bible! In it are found the answers to the wailings of the existentialist, the gropings of the philosopher, the inquiries of the scholar. There also is found the "historical Jesus" some seek.

Only in the Scriptures are revealed the eternal truths of Christ, who he was and what he did. It is not human reason that makes these things plain; rather, faith accepts them as revealed. God has revealed himself in the Person of his Son so that, seeing him, we know what God is like. Human reason can never account for Christ; only faith apprehends him.

To those who will see and hear, God also reveals himself through the presence and power of the Holy Spirit. It is he who takes the things of Christ and through them speaks to our hearts and minds. To the unregenerate mind, the person and work of the Holy Spirit are incomprehensible.

Every revelation from God and of God must be accepted by faith. The great emphasis of the New Testament is on faith. It is to those who believe, not those who employ mere human reason, that Christ becomes a living Saviour. The foolishness of the Cross saves those who subordinate human intellectual concepts to God's divine wisdom. To try to reason and rationalize the meaning of our Lord's death on Calvary can lead only to folly. To accept it by faith is to bring the wisdom and understanding of God into one's soul.

Of course reason has its place, but it is not enough in itself. It must be aided by revelation and enlightened by faith.

I see an apple by the side of the road, and reason tells me there is an apple tree somewhere. But only revelation tells me where the tree came from.

I read the morning paper with its stories of war and suffering, crime and lust, injustices and oppression. Reason tells me that there is something wrong with the world. Only revelation tells me that it is sin in the human heart and that sin is disobedience to God's holy laws.

And revelation goes further. It tells of God's remedy for man's predicament. It tells me of the things that are seen and those that are not seen and of their comparative values.

Giving priority to revelation rather than to human reason takes humility, the "faith of a little child" of which our Lord spoke. This is not childishness but the subordination of human wisdom to the wisdom of God, so that our boast is not in man but in God.

Once the demand of revelation over human reason is recognized, faith itself becomes reasonable. Supernatural Christianity (e.g., the Incarnation and the Virgin Birth) becomes truly reasonable when received through the eye of faith. Until there is faith, all that is miraculous and supernatural is foolishness. Once a man recognizes that God in his dealings and manifestations transcends human reason and experience, he finds that faith itself commends as reasonable that about which the world knows nothing.

Many of the problems of theology and of the Church arise through a sophistication that is an enemy of Christianity. When reason divorced from faith is given top priority, faith shrivels. The Bible teaches that "no wisdom, no understanding, no counsel, can avail against the Lord" (Prov. 21:30). It is equally explicit in saying that because "the world did not know God through wisdom, it pleased God through the folly of what we preach to save those who believe" (I Cor. 1:21). The gateway to eternal life lies not in human reason but in the divine revelation of Jesus Christ and all that is implied by his death and resurrection. The Gospel centers in these two historical facts.

Reasonable? Only to those who know by faith the truth of God's revelation.

I plead with you . . .

GIVE IT A CHANCE

Millions inside and outside the Church are spiritually ignorant, emotionally insecure, frustrated, and unhappy. But their
lives can be completely transformed. Spiritual understanding can replace ignorance. A sense of security can come,
bringing emotional stability. Peace can take the place of
frustration. And an inner joy can settle in that the world
cannot take away.

How can a person experience such a change? By reading
the Bible, taking it at its word, and receiving the Christ it
reveals.

I have written on this subject before and will probably do
so again, because I am convinced that people—Christians
above all others—are missing a blessing beyond anything they
have ever known by failing to make the Bible a daily com-
panion.

Oh, I know all about the tired old charge that we "worship"
the Bible. It is hardly worthy of reply. The surgeon does
not worship his knife and diagnostic equipment—but he trusts
and uses them. The artist does not worship his brushes and
oils, but he relies on them to produce the effects he desires.

Studying the Bible with a simple faith in its integrity and authority brings a reward achieved in no other way—the assurance that God is speaking to one's heart and life.

Why not give the Bible a chance to speak? All other books, even the best of them, are men's books and the expression of men's wisdom. The Bible is God's book, the expression of God's wisdom. In it one can find the answers to the questions and uncertainties of life. Its message provides assurance that will banish fear from the heart and mind.

One of the most amazing things about the Bible is its relevance. It is more up to date than tomorrow's newspaper, for it accurately tells of the future. It is wholly relevant in the moral realm, also, because since the beginning of time man's basic problems have been the same. His sins have always been the same. The Bible is God's word to man, and God never changes. He always stands ready to meet every need.

American business is based on proving the worth of one's product. Advertising, samples, testimonials all have their place. I am simply asking that you give the Bible a chance to prove that it can bring a new dimension into your life.

Of primary importance is the Christ revealed in both the Old and the New Testament. In the Bible we learn of his Person and his work—that he is the Son of God, and that, for the believer, he is Saviour and Lord.

The earnest seeker will find within the pages of this book a philosophy for living and also for dying. The Bible is a book by a Friend that tells us about a Friend. God speaks through all its pages. In the Old Testament we find history and the whys and wherefores of matters that have perplexed the wisest. We also find poetry, inspired by the Holy Spirit, that puts into words the deepest feelings and longings of the human heart. And we find prophecy, which tells of the coming of the Christ as suffering servant and his return as triumphant King and Judge.

Many have lost all sense of awe and reverence for Scripture because they have come to view it as a "human document" that can be understood only by those who can analyze its origins and history. Some are like the curious child who picks apart a rose to find out where the beauty and fragrance come from and in so doing destroys the rose.

I have known too many people whose joy and confidence in the Bible has been undermined by those who dissect it with a critical and unbelieving heart or who accept scholarly "findings" that, in their eyes, discredit its integrity and authority.

For many of us this book is the *Holy* Bible; but, sad to say, for many others it is only exceptionally good literature, subject to the frailties of the human mind and limited by the ignorance of the writers.

There seems to be a strange fascination in the minds of some, a determination to "interpret" the Bible on the sole basis of human scholarship. This scholarship *starts* with the presupposition that one is dealing with a human document, not a supernatural one. As a result its "interpretations" frankly deny the clear statements of Scripture. This is not "intepretation" but utter presumption.

Much is said against the practice of "literalism" in interpreting the Bible, but more needs to be said about denials of the unequivocal statements of Scripture in the name of "scholarship" and "recently discovered manuscripts." The fact remains, that not one manuscript has ever been discovered that in any way invalidates the basic doctrines of Christianity. We must be wary of a pseudo-scholarship that seems willing, even glad, to deny the honest interpretation of the Word of God.

Let those who are confused because of the limitations and interpretations of men turn to the Bible. Let it speak for itself! It will speak to your heart, appeal to your mind, command your will.

I am convinced of the reality and astuteness of Satan. And I am equally convinced that in no area is he more active today than in turning men away from the Bible. The question in the Garden, "Yea, hath God said?," is still heard in many places. The "If you are . . ." suggestions of Satan in the wilderness continue to plague men. We need to utter the words of affirmation: "I believe; help my unbelief" (Mark 9:24, RSV). "Let God be true though every man be false . . ." (Rom. 3:4); "All scripture is inspired by God . . ." (II Tim. 3:16); "No prophecy ever came by the impulse of man, but men moved by the Holy Spirit spoke from God" (II Pet. 1:21).

Give the Bible a chance. Let it speak to you, knowing that it is God who speaks in words the hungry and believing heart can understand. Let no man stand between you and God's Word. Give the Bible a chance to speak for itself, and the Holy Spirit who moved the hearts of men to speak for God will interpret its meaning to you and bring a faith, comfort, and hope that nothing and no one can dispel.

Use several translations or versions if you prefer. A few years ago a prominent American had become interested in studying the Bible, but about that time a furor arose over the Revised Standard Version, and in disgust he gave up his study. No translation is perfect (the King James Version certainly is not); yet in any translation and any language there breathes forth the fact that this is not a human document but God's Word. If God has spoken, how important it is that we find out what he has to say!

Let us not rest on what men say; let God speak for himself. Give the Bible a chance in your heart, and God will do the rest.

*One looks at much going on today in the
name of the Church
and can but wonder whether it is . . .*

RELEVANT OR IRRELEVANT?

Much is being said to the effect that the Church is no longer
being relevant to the world in which we live. Only recently
I heard a prominent entertainer say that the Church has
no meaning to young people because it has no answers, either
for their personal problems or for the problems of the world.

Where this is actually the case, may not the reason be that
the modern Church is abandoning its God-ordained role in
the world to become involved in areas to which it is not
called and for which its leaders are not qualified?

The Church is truly relevant only when it faithfully witnesses to a message—a message from God to man; when it
gives itself to the preaching, teaching, and living of Christ, the
one and only Mediator between God and man; when its primary concern is to point men to God's Son as Saviour from sin
and Lord of life.

It becomes utterly irrelevant when it preaches a Christ
who is not the Christ of the Bible but has been divested of
his supernatural and miraculous nature; when its primary
concern is with the condition of the Prodigal in the Far Coun-

try, trying to make him happy, comfortable, and prosperous rather than to bring him home to his Father; when its leadership has shifted from a spiritual task to one that is largely political, economic, and social.

The Church is rendered ineffectual and irrelevant when it cuts loose from the anchor of faith in the Holy Scriptures and substitutes for that faith an attitude of criticism of divine revelation, setting up its programs with little or no reference to the plain teachings of that revelation. This becomes an ever increasing problem as seminaries turn out more and more men who have no idea of preaching the Gospel but rather use their training and calling for secular ends.

What could work more against effective leadership than catering to the changing foibles of a "lost generation" instead of offering them a faith to follow, a living Christ to believe in?

I am convinced that the turmoil among young people today has come about largely because we elders have failed them and the Church has failed them. Our homes, churches, and schools are so materialistically oriented, our outlook so fixed on the immediate situation in the world, that young people are crying in vain for something to satisfy their spiritual hunger, though they are not sure what it is they want.

We have lost them in the home by failing to place Christ at the center of every phase of life, and in the Church by increasingly emphasizing this world and its problems without reference to the solutions found alone in Christ. Our schools have become entirely secular and, under the guise of a separation of education from all religious influences, have in fact become hotbeds of anti-God and anti-Christian teaching.

In shifting the emphasis from the central to peripheral and secondary matters, the Church seems to have forgotten that it is possible to gain the whole world and yet lose one's soul. It has apparently forgotten that man does not live by bread alone, and that God has faithfully promised to supply every material need if we will put him first in our lives.

In its search for contemporary relevance, let the Church acknowledge that neither science nor human achievement in any realm has changed the nature of man one whit. The human heart is the same today as in the day of Noah, when "the earth was corrupt in God's sight, and the earth was filled with violence" (Gen. 6:11), or the time when our Lord himself observed that "out of the heart come evil thoughts, murder, adultery, fornication, theft, false witness, slander. These are what defile a man" (Matt. 15:19, 20a).

The Church must face up to the question of sin in the human heart and God's remedy for that sin; it must abandon the attempt to wash the outside of the cup with no thought of the rottenness inside.

Man and this world must be viewed in the light of eternity. In the words of the Apostle Paul, we must "look not to the things that are seen but to the things that are unseen; for the things that are seen are transient, but the things that are unseen are eternal" (II Cor. 4:18).

To put it as clearly as possible: The Church is relevant when it recognizes its spiritual calling, message, and mission, and irrelevant when it attempts to become an agency for social reform.

To the immediate rejoinder that the Church belies its calling if it is not concerned about the plight of men enmeshed in poverty, blighted by discrimination, and suffering from the age-old problem of man's inhumanity to man, let me say that it is the Christian's duty to be concerned about these things and to use every legitimate means to help. A Christian without compassion in his heart is unworthy of the name he bears. A Christian who does not translate compassion into works of mercy is like those who passed by on the other side in our Lord's story of the Good Samaritan.

But Christians do not just happen. They are people who have come into a vital personal relationship with Jesus Christ. By accepting him as Saviour and making him Lord of life, they themselves become "salt" in a festering society and "light" in a darkened world. This is the Church's primary task.

The social order will never be changed by pronouncements of church courts; nor should the Church, in the name of the Church, hope to change it merely through programs of reform.

It is impossible to effect any great or lasting change in society without first changing the hearts of those who compose it. And who but the Church has the necessary message of personal redemption? What other organization is called to summon men to be reconciled to God through faith in his Son and then to be reconciled one to another through the living presence of the Holy Spirit in their lives?

But one is forced to the reluctant conclusion that many who would speak for the Church no longer hold to those basic matters of the Christian faith that have made it separate and distinct from the world order. The transition from spiritual death to spiritual life, which our Lord called being born again, centers in and depends on faith in Jesus Christ as Son of God—crucified, buried, and risen from the dead.

Also involved is the question of conviction of sin, repentance for sin, and conversion. Why is so little said about repentance today, even though Jesus made it a prerequisite for salvation? In fact, why is so little being said about salvation? The only possible explanation is that many who are speaking for the Church no longer believe in the relevance of Jesus Christ for man's predicament.

Where the Church is irrelevant to the world and its needs, the reason must be it has lost its vision and its message.

In the world today man can find . . .

LIGHT IN DARKNESS

Imagine yourself in an unlighted house on a dark night. There are other people there, and you hear a crash as someone stumbles into a piece of furniture and a resounding bump as another runs blindly into a wall. Then there is a series of thuds, accompanied by cries of pain, as someone falls down an unseen stairway.

The cause of all the trouble is obvious: people are groping around in darkness. Light is not available—no one has found the switch.

Read this morning's newspaper, any newspaper, anywhere. You read of confusion, strife, warfare, crime, violence. You read of human misery and degradation. It is a sordid and distressing picture that rejects the world as it is and the people in the world as they are.

But the cause of the world's sorrows and trouble is not diagnosed by the world's leaders, nor by the news media. The cause is spiritual darkness, spiritual blindness. Those unable to see are acting as guides. Those in distress see neither the immediate reason for their trouble nor the underlying condition that makes that trouble inevitable.

One day Jesus said to his disciples, "I am the light of the world; he who follows me will not walk in darkness, but will have the light of life" (John 8:12). We Christians tend to think we are in a privileged category that carries with it light for today and hope for tomorrow. And we are. We *do* have light for today and hope for tomorrow. We *do* see the world in a perspective unknown to those who are not Christians. We *can* diagnose the cause of world disorder and know the answer to the problem. But ability to diagnose and knowledge of the answer implies that we ourselves must do something about it. And it is precisely at this point that many of us fail.

For Jesus also said, "You [believers] are the light of the world." He did not say that this is an inherent light; it is a reflected one, the light of Jesus Christ shining in and through the lives of those whom he has gloriously redeemed.

Our Lord compared Christians with "a city set on a hill," which cannot be hid. Christians are to be in the world not as enclaves of the saved but as witnesses to others. Jesus went on to say, "Nor do men light a lamp and put it under a bushel, but on a stand, and it gives light to all in the house" (Matt. 5:15).

Perhaps far more than we realize we Christians have been oblivious to our duty to shine as lights in an otherwise dark place. This is not an obscure theological problem but one of intense daily significance. People do not see Jesus in person; they see him reflected in the lives of those who have been redeemed by him. They should see in us love where others hate, a love for the unlovely as well as the lovely. They should see in our lives a joy that has its wellsprings in the living Christ. They should see evidence of a peaceful heart, one in which there dwells the peace of God because there is peace *with* God.

Those around us should find in us patience under provocation, kindness and compassion for those in need, faithfulness and gentleness and self-control. The light of Christ, which shines through his own, is in sharp contrast to spiritual darkness.

Jesus laid down the rule of life for Christians in the command, "Let your light so shine before men, that they may see your good works and give glory to your Father who is in heaven" (Matt. 5:16). In the past twenty-four hours, have I shone as a light in a dark place? Have you?

Christianity is an intensely practical matter. Revelation, history, doctrine? Yes, all these. But Christianity is, above all, Jesus Christ, and (because of him) Christian people in whom there exists the life and love of the Saviour, and in whose hearts there is the light of eternity. We who name the name of Christ should validate our faith by showing a quality of life alien to this world, thereby being an effective witness.

The Apostle Paul wrote to a small band of Christians, his first converts in Europe, living in the midst of a growing area of transcontinental commerce and surrounded by pagan beliefs and practices. They had survived as a Christian group despite the pressures of their times, but Paul wanted them to do more. They were to be beacon lights in the midst of the darkness of a culture alienated from God. He wrote, "Do all things without grumbling or questioning, that you may be blameless and innocent, children of God without blemish in the midst of a crooked and perverse generation, among whom you shine as lights in the world, holding fast the word of life" (Phil. 2:14–16a).

They were not to lead a pietistic life of physical separation from those about them. But they were to be blameless and innocent of worldy contamination, leading pure and good lives that would be a rebuke to the crookedness and perverseness all around them.

We who believe in the saving and keeping power of Jesus Christ, *must,* if we are to let our light shine for his glory, guard our actions, words, and thoughts. How do we act in the face of temptation? When challenged by hard choices, what do we choose? In our contacts with those who do not know Christ, do we love them for his sake?

There is always the temptation to cloister ourselves with those with whom we can enjoy spiritual fellowship. There is the further temptation to draw about us the steely robes of self-righteousness and in so doing create an impenetrable barrier between us and the very ones who most need our message. Men may reject the light of the Gospel—but what a tragedy when Christians give no evidence of its presence in their lives, either by word or by deed!

Perhaps there is no place where we Christians need more to practice self-examination than right here. At the end of the day, ask yourself whether you have let your light shine for the glory of God. Review the day before going to sleep, and let the Holy Spirit convict you of carrying a darkened lantern, if this is what you have done.

And at the start of each day, we should pray for the love and grace we need to give unmistakable evidence that we are Christians and that we want others to find the same joy and hope we have.

Countless eyes watch us. What do they see? The Ephesian Christians lived in a city noted for its wickedness. To them the Apostle Paul wrote, "For though once your heart was full of darkness, now it is full of light from the Lord, and your behavior should show it" (Eph. 5:8, *Living Letters*).

Is your light showing?

The whole matter is . . .

VERY PERSONAL

Many of us are convinced that it is impossible to reform the social order apart from the personal redemption of individuals. We will be wise if we carry the same line of reasoning into our concept of the work of the Holy Spirit in individuals and in the Church.

We are inclined to think of his work in general and impersonal terms. We pray for an "outpouring of the Holy Spirit," as if he worked in some nebulous way apart from the lives of people. True, he may use things and events for his glory and the advancement of God's Kingdom; but he possesses and fills *people* and works through them.

The very heart of the Christian faith is man's personal relationship with God. Man stands before God as an individual, and as an individual he is redeemed. The work of the Holy Spirit is personal. It is he who effects the new birth, who brings spiritual life from spiritual death. It is he who comes into the hearts and lives, wooing, speaking of the things of Christ, and instructing in spiritual truth.

When the Holy Spirit came at Pentecost, there were supernatural manifestations that immediately became personalized.

The "tongues of fire," we are told, were "distributed and resting on each one of them. And they were all filled with the Holy Spirit . . ." (Acts 2:3, 4, RSV). And because this experience was personalized, these unlearned Galileans went out transformed.

The phrase "a Spirit-filled Church" can be misleading. It is the persons making up the Church who must be filled with the Spirit, and we cannot avoid this necessity by thinking or hoping that God works in some other way.

There is no doctrine more neglected than that of the Holy Spirit. Much is said about God the Father, and about his Son, the Lord Jesus Christ, and of course none of us can fully understand or exhaust these subjects. But about the Holy Spirit there is abysmal ignorance and often a strange indifference. Yet it is he by whom alone we can believe in Christ and be prepared to witness for him. It is through the Holy Spirit that the Bible becomes an open book. The Holy Spirit is not an accessory to Christian faith and work; *he is a necessity*.

Most churches are today confronted with a depressing fact: the spiritual birthrate increasingly lags behind the biological. In desperation we turn to new programs and new methods. Some even attempt to jettison basic parts of the Christian faith in favor of ideas more acceptable to the unregenerate. How foolish can we get?

If there is to be a change—and there can be—we must search our own hearts for the cause of the trouble. Is there concrete evidence of the presence and power of the Holy Spirit *in us?* There can be no improvement in the general situation in the Church until there is a change in the lives of individual Christians, in the pulpit as well as in the pew. An answer to the problem is a personal one; it affects you and me.

Confronted as we are with spiritual deadness in the Church,

let us honestly admit that this deadness lies within us as individuals. The Church's state is an elongated shadow of the state of its members. And the great omission in its members' lives is the failure to recognize the absolute necessity of a personal experience with the Holy Spirit—an experience that transforms and quickens, not the organization, but the people who make up that organization.

We thrill at the story of Pentecost and perhaps are inclined to look on it merely as a phenomenon in history. But the coming of the Holy Spirit in mighty power in the lives of Christians should be a continuing experience within the Church.

The significance of the manifestation at Pentecost was not that rude fishermen were suddenly able to speak in other languages. Rather, it was that they were transformed into something they had not been previously. Only a few days before they had been scattered, and one of their number had denied his Lord before a mere servant maid. Then, when filled with the Spirit, this same man stood fearlessly before the Sanhedrin, who had condemned Christ, and boldly denounced them for their sin while pleading with them to repent. Even these enemies of our Lord recognized that the disciples had been with Jesus and, at this time, dismissed them with nothing more than a threat.

Obviously, the Holy Spirit changes the person in whom he lives. It is by his presence that men become "new creatures" in Christ. But how often do we see any vital change today? The lack of evidence of transformed lives rests as a dead weight on the Church and discredits the validity of the Christian faith in the eyes of an unbelieving world.

The change that takes place is a tremendous one. The fruits of the indwelling Spirit, enumerated by Paul in Galatians 5:22, 23, are the result of a supernatural work, contrary to man's natural behavior. Do we by our own lives show these fruits to others? Do we have a consciousness of love, joy, and peace within?

These are questions we need to answer in all honesty. In the answer, either spiritual health or sickness—even to death—is indicated.

Our Lord described the work of the Spirit to Nicodemus as something to be felt. We cannot see the wind, but we feel its effect. So it is with the Spirit of God. There *must be* an effect of his presence in our lives, felt by us and seen by others.

This change and empowering is a constant work of the Holy Spirit, renewed day by day in the hearts and lives of those who turn to him. It is through such persons that the Christian witness is made effective.

Recently I heard a successful young minister speak about "communicating" the Gospel. He wisely observed, "I cannot communicate the Gospel, nor can any one else. It is the Holy Spirit alone who makes the Gospel intelligible to people."

Perhaps many of our failures stem from misapprehensions about this vital matter. We are prone to depend on personality, education, organizational structure, and programs as the primary means of leading people to believe. Important and useful as all of these may be, they are useless unless surrendered to the leading and power of the Holy Spirit. God has used some very unlikely people and methods, while some grandiose, expensive, and sophisticated methods have failed miserably. The word of the Lord to Zerubbabel holds good today: "Not by might, nor by power, but by my Spirit, says the Lord of hosts" (Zech. 4:6).

The Holy Spirit is no longer the dominant reality in many churches because he is no longer the dominant reality in the members' own personal lives. This is a serious spiritual situation, the cause of weakness and ineffectiveness.

Things do not have to continue as they are, however. There can be a tremendous change, a new surge of power and understanding, a new sense of urgency for a world that has gone far down the road to destruction.

This change must take place in a person's heart and mind, and it is possible only by the in-filling of the Holy Spirit. God has promised to give his Spirit to those who ask him. His presence will open up an entirely new concept of what it means to be a Christian. We, and the Church, can then become filled with life and power—God living in us.

It will make all the difference!

Man desperately needs . . .

WISDOM FROM ABOVE

"The fear of the LORD is the beginning of wisdom, and the knowledge of the Holy One is insight" (Prov. 9:10, RSV).

According to this description, many of the world's "wise" ones have never come out of kindergarten and into the realities of life.

If true wisdom is the orientation of self and the affairs of this world to the Creator-Redeemer, how many of us possess it? Only the fool says God does not exist (Ps. 14:1). The wise man gives God his rightful place in every realm—creation, history, and destiny—and recognizes him as sovereign over individuals and over nations.

Such wisdom, coming as it does from a reverential fear of and trust in God, produces peace, joy, and hope, independent of outward circumstances. It is the preventative for the situation our Lord described as "men fainting with fear and with foreboding of what is coming on the world . . ." (Luke 21:26).

Even for believers it is usually true that their God is too small. Like the timid souls of every generation, we tend to conceive of God as being bound by our own limitations. Thus we view life with a sense of futility.

To combat this we should pray for and foster in our own hearts and minds a concept of God that reaches back into eternity, outward into infinity, and forward to a joyous and unending life with him. The eternal sovereignty of God, once it is grasped, lifts our hearts and enlightens our minds; and when with this we envision something of the awesome reality of his love, glory, and power, we are on the way to being wise—as God counts wisdom.

When we are able to say with the Psalmist, "For I know that the LORD is great, and that our LORD is above all gods. Whatever the LORD pleases he does, in heaven and on earth, in the seas and all deeps" (Ps. 135:5, 6), we find that life comes into clear focus. Doubts vanish when we realize that "the LORD [who] by wisdom founded the earth; by understanding . . . established the heavens" (Prov. 3:19) is the same Lord who came to redeem us from our sins.

Christians lose much joy in life by failing to recognize that the God of creation is also the God of history. As such he is sovereign also in love and in judgment. We have nothing to fear, for the wrath of a holy God against sin has been borne in the person of his Son.

On one hand there is redeeming love. On the other there is consuming judgment. The Prophet Isaiah speaks of the latter: "I will punish the world for its evil, and the wicked for their iniquity; I will put an end to the pride of the arrogant, and lay low the haughtiness of the ruthless. I will make men more rare than fine gold, and mankind than the gold of Ophir. Therefore I will make the heavens tremble, and the earth will be shaken out of its place, at the wrath of the LORD of hosts in the day of his fierce anger" (Isa. 13:11–13).

The Prophet Jeremiah too had a vision of the God of

history. He wrote, "Thus says the Lord of hosts, the God of Israel: . . . It is I who by my great power and my outstretched arm have made the earth, with the men and animals that are on the earth, and I give it to whomever it seems right to me" (Jer. 27:4b, 5).

Writing of Israel's apostasy and sinfulness, the Apostle Paul says, "Now these things happened to them as a warning, but they were written down for our instruction, upon whom the end of the ages has come" (I Cor. 10:11).

The wisdom God gives to those who fear him puts him on the throne in every area of his universe—in creation, in history, and also in destiny. He who brought the world into existence will surely control the course of events to the end. Today we see the rage and tumult of men and nations. Has God been dethroned? Has he abdicated? Has he lost control of events? Far from it. No circumstances of our individual lives, no courses of nations, are completed until God has finished his own work in and through them.

Man's greatest folly is to lift himself, the creature, above the Creator. That many deny or ignore God only adds to their guilt. Materialism in every age has been concerned with the tangible. Only by the wisdom God gives can men see beyond the horizon and on into eternity. Then and only then can time and eternity come into proper perspective.

The wisdom of this world enables man to discover the facts of the universe, but only the wisdom that is from above can bring us to know the eternal Source of all things. And to know Him is life eternal.

It is by faith that we become wise, for faith, the basis of godly wisdom, rests on intangibles (by worldly standards) that are real only to those who believe. The love of a mother may be called an intangible, but it is wonderfully real. So the wisdom God imparts to those who believe in him brings reality out of unreality and gives substance to things the world can never see.

The fear of the Lord, which is the beginning of wisdom, is God's gift to the humble. A childlike attitude of mind is the gateway to God's grace. It is not a mere lazy acquiescence but a rational acknowledgment of God as Creator and Lord.

The humble heart knows its need. It comes to see itself in the light of God's holiness and to admit with the Prophet Jeremiah, "The heart is deceitful above all things, and desperately corrupt . . ." (Jer. 17:9). Such humility recognizes that "before him no creature is hidden, but all are open and laid bare to the eyes of him with whom we have to do" (Heb. 4:13).

The inescapable link between true wisdom and genuine humility rests in the *perspective* this wisdom gives. When we see ourselves in the light of God's holiness, we are inclined to cry out with Job, "I had heard of thee by the hearing of the ear, but now my eye sees thee; therefore I despise myself, and repent in dust and ashes" (Job 42:5, 6). Thomas showed true wisdom and humility when he cried, "My Lord and my God" (John 20:28).

Only the Spirit of God can enable us to see the vast gulf between wisdom and knowledge. The Apostle Paul aptly says that "knowledge puffs up." Wisdom enables man to use knowledge for God's glory. That secular knowledge is exalted above wisdom is one aspect of the spiritual blindness of unregenerate man. There can be no true wisdom apart from God.

The writer of the Book of Proverbs admonishes, "Get wisdom, and whatever you get, get insight" (Prov. 4:7). Is not the lack of such insight the cause of much of the chaotic thinking and living today?

The frustration, uncertainty, and fear we see on every hand

can be exchanged for peace, certainty, and perfect assurance if we appropriate the wisdom God yearns to give. This is the Christian's privilege and at the same time his opportunity. All about us are people who are educated, perhaps, but who lack true wisdom because there is no fear of God in their hearts.

Christians become . . .

SUPERNATURALIZED CITIZENS

We have all heard about people who are said to be "so heavenly minded that they are of no earthly use." Perhaps there are a few such people. But most of those in this world—many Christians among them—are so wrapped up in the things of this earth that they have no time for heaven or eternal values.

The Christian should realize that he has changed his citizenship. In praying for his disciples, our Lord said, "I do not pray that thou shouldst take them out of the world, but that thou shouldst keep them from the evil one. They are not of the world, even as I am not of the world" (John 17:15, 16, RSV).

When the seventy returned from their mission, they were rejoicing that even the demons were subject to the name of Jesus. The Lord's reply was, "Do not rejoice in this, that the spirits are subject to you; but rejoice that your names are written in heaven" (Luke 10:20).

Speaking of the heroes of faith, the writer of the Epistle to the Hebrews says, "These all died in faith, not having received what was promised, but having seen it and greeted it from afar, and having acknowledged that they were strangers and exiles on the earth. For people who speak thus make it clear that they are seeking a homeland. If they had been thinking of that land from which they had gone out, they would have opportunity to return. But as it is, they desire a better country, that is, a heavenly one. Therefore God is not ashamed to be called their God, for he has prepared for them a city" (Heb. 11:13–16).

Moses, the same writer says, "refused to be called the son of Pharaoh's daughter, choosing rather to share ill-treatment with the people of God than to enjoy the fleeting pleasures of sin. . . . He endured as seeing him who is invisible" (vv. 25, 27b).

And Abraham "went out, not knowing where he was to go. . . . For he looked forward to the city which has foundations, whose builder and maker is God" (vv. 8b, 10).

Christians need to know the place of their spiritual citizenship. It helps clarify many problems and prevent unnecessary frustrations.

But being a Christian involves far more than a heavenly citizenship; it also involves living as a Christian in this world. It means being the very best kind of citizen. It means showing the fruits of the Holy Spirit in daily relationships with other people. It includes not only love for God but also love for our fellow man. We should be concerned for our neighbor's best interests as if they were our own.

Almost immediately after our Lord affirmed the heavenly citizenship of those who believe on him, he spoke of their earthly obligation to others through the story of the Good Samaritan. No degree of heavenly involvement can absolve us from our responsibility to be good neighbors.

What then, is the proper balance in the life of one who is a citizen of two worlds, so to speak?

Balance is established, first of all, by a firm footing. We can maintain a right relation with God and with man only by standing firm on Jesus Christ, the immovable foundation. There can be no right relation with men unless there is a right relation with God, and no man can attain this merely by being a good neighbor. Rather, he becomes a good neighbor by receiving Christ into his own heart. Then and only then is it possible for him to love his neighbor as himself.

This effective balance in life is the result of God's grace in the human heart. It is God who puts life in proper perspective. He speaks to us in his Word about how to live with and for others and how to glorify him.

In the same prayer in which our Lord speaks to believers as being in but not of the world, he also speaks of "eternal life" as a gift and as a right apprehension of God through Christ.

The esoteric nature of this prayer is most enlightening, particularly when so many today are placing believers and unbelievers in the same category: "I am praying for them; I am not praying for the world but for those whom thou hast given me, for they are thine" (John 17:9).

And then we read this remarkable and deeply significant statement, "I have given them thy word; and the world has hated them because they are not of the world, even as I am not of the world" (v. 14).

Were the disciples to rest in their assurance of eternal life and from then on merely wait for their translation into the heavenly Kingdom? Far from it. They had a message to proclaim, a work to do. Their lives would not be easy. They would be rejected as he had been rejected. They were to be witnesses because they had been with him from the beginning. Some hearers would believe the message; many others would reject it.

The life of the believer is that of a messenger with a

message. Because he lives in an unbelieving world, one that crucified the Lord of glory and would crucify him again if he were here today in the flesh, the Christian must expect hostility toward himself and toward the Gospel he lives and preaches. "If the world hates you, know that it has hated me before it hated you. If you were of the world, the world would love its own; but because you are not of the world, but I chose you out of the world, therefore the world hates you" (John 15:18, 19).

The Christian's reaction to hostility must be one of love. For this our Lord has set the perfect example. Paul speaks to the problem: "The Lord's servant must not be quarrelsome but kindly to every one, an apt teacher, forbearing, correcting his opponents with gentleness. God may perhaps grant that they will repent and come to know the truth, and they may escape from the snare of the devil, after being captured by him to do his will" (II Tim. 2:24).

As a citizen of heaven, the Christian lives in enemy territory. He is involved in deadly warfare. He is up against, not a physical enemy, but "the unseen power that controls this dark world, and spiritual agents from the very headquarters of evil" (Eph. 6:12b, Phillips). In his own strength and with his own resources he is helpless.

But the battle is not lost. God has provided his own with an armor against which Satan's wiles are useless. He has provided the one offensive weapon against which Satan can never stand, "the Sword of the Spirit, which is the word of God."

Where so many of us fail as heavenly citizens is in our attempt to fight with carnal weapons—criticism, invective, worldly wisdom, and a host of other things that are of the flesh, and not of the Spirit.

The Apostle Paul has put our citizenship and inevitable

warfare in perfect perspective with his words in Second Corinthians 10:3, 4—"Though we live in the world we are not carrying on a worldly war, for the weapons of our warfare are not worldly but have divine power to destroy strongholds."

True Christianity develops certain . . .

DISTINCTIVES OF THE CHRISTIAN LIFE

The world needs to see lives that have been transformed by Jesus Christ. This does not mean that true Christians are popular with the world. The Apostle Paul makes it plain that the opposite is true: "All who desire to live a godly life in Christ Jesus will be persecuted" (II Tim. 3:12).

Paul also describes the kind of life the Christian should live in the environment the world provides: "that you may be blameless and innocent, children of God without blemish in the midst of a crooked and perverse generation, among whom you shine as lights in the world, holding fast the word of life" (Phil. 2:15, 16*a*).

How can we live such a life? How can the distinctives of Christian character be nurtured?

A Christian is one who has accepted Jesus Christ as Saviour and who should have made him Lord of life. But we all know from experience and from observation that there are vast differences among those who profess the name of Christ, even though the goal of all Christians should be to honor and glorify Christ in everything they do.

What explains these differences? What can we do to reflect in our outward life the fullness of the indwelling Saviour?

A true believer in Christ is indwelt and empowered by his Spirit. The Bible is explicit in telling us of the fruit of the Spirit: "love, joy, peace, patience, kindness, goodness, faithfulness, gentleness, and self-control."

Let's be honest and objective. As we search our own lives, can we say that we have the internal and external evidence of the fruit of the Holy Spirit? If not, let us see what the Bible teaches about the Holy Spirit and then seek his fullness and blessings in our hearts and lives.

Strong convictions are a part of Christian character. We must realize the difference, however, between legitimate convictions and personal prejudices. We must be sure that our convictions are based on an understanding of the Word of God rather than on our own or others' opinions.

A Christian must have a very clear understanding of the nature and reality of sin. He must realize that basically sin is disobedience to the revealed will of God. In all of us there is the pull of the world, the flesh, and the Devil, encouraging us to think and do wrong things.

At all times Satan stands ready to entice us to evil, tempt us to do wrong, accuse us to God, and lead us astray. Paul speaks of him as "the unseen power that controls this dark world" and mentions also "spiritual agents from the very headquarters of evil" (Eph. 6:12, Phillips). To deny the reality of Satan is to court disaster. We are in the grimmest of warfares, with much at stake.

But the Christian has no right to be a pessimist. The One who has forgiven and cleansed us has made *complete* provision, not only for the sins of the past, but also for the living of each day in victory in him. He remembers that we are weak and sinful, and he always offers forgiveness with the promise of life in a new dimension. All we need do is claim these things he is so willing to give us.

In the heart of each Christian there should be a spiritual compass, an understanding of the difference between right and wrong. There should be a recognition of the validity of God's moral law. Just as there are natural and physical laws that continue to be valid from one generation to another, so too there are unchanging moral and spiritual laws.

The Ten Commandments continue to be God's revelation of these principles. No man has ever kept them perfectly, nor can any do so; and our salvation does not depend on their being kept. But through these messages given on Sinai we gain an understanding of man's duty to God and to his fellow man. Christ summarized the Commandments in these words: "You shall love the Lord your God with all your heart, and with all your soul, and with all your mind. This is the great and first commandment. And a second is like it, You shall love your neighbor as yourself. On these two commandments depend all the law and the prophets" (Matt. 22:37–40).

If we recognize God's right to set spiritual and moral standards and his gift of his Son through whom we can live by these standards, it follows that we should surrender our hearts, minds, and wills to him. It is a matter not only of faith but also of obedience, for faith without obedience is not true faith.

One element in the Christian character that stands out clearly to others is the unwillingness to compromise on a principle. The Prophet Isaiah lived in discouraging times when there was compromise with evil on every hand. In the midst of it all he remained true to God: "For the Lord GOD helps me; . . . therefore I have set my face like a flint, and I know

that I shall not be put to shame; he who vindicates me is near"
(Isa. 50:7, 8a).

Every Christian should, like Isaiah, live in close communion
with and obedience to God. This is achieved by trusting
God and using the means of grace he has given. Without
prayer and faithful Bible study, no Christian can live as he
should. Failure to be informed and instructed in the things
revealed in God's word leads to certain defeat.

Every Christian should live with confidence, hope, and
assurance, not in himself but in the faithfulness and goodness
of God. God does not expect anything of us for which he has
not made provision. He knows we are weak, and so he has
provided the strength. He knows we will be tempted, and he
has provided the way of escape. He knows we are ignorant,
and he has provided the necessary wisdom. He knows we
are easily confused, and he has provided light to show the
way in which we should walk.

To live as Christians should, we must live humbly, always
remembering that, but for the love, grace, and mercy of God
we would be lost. There is no place for pride or self-satis-
faction. Everything we have now and for eternity we have
through the One who died in our place and for our sins, who
took our punishment, and who makes us righteous in God's
sight.

The more clearly we realize that we, as Christians, have
been freed from the sentence of death and are free to give
praise to God, the more surely we will live as Christians
should.

We have been redeemed because of his amazing grace;
nothing less than undying love should be our response.

*Despite the world around him the
Christian can pass from . . .*

CONFUSION TO TRANQUILLITY

Nothing reflects confusion more than a flock of sheep without
a shepherd. Beset by barking dogs, frustrated by one another
and by the natural obstacles around them, leaderless sheep
will mill about in a frenzy of indecision; unable to cope with
the problems that confront them.

That the world of men is in a like state of confusion is seen
in even the most casual reading of any newspaper. The
problems are economic, racial, political, and social. They are
also educational, emotional, and—above all—spiritual.

Each geographical area has its own problems, with resulting alignments and counter-alignments that jeopardize local
and world peace.

For the world's confusion, as for each man's confusion,
there has been committed to the church and to individual
Christians a simple and direct answer. This answer, which can
be either accepted or rejected, forms the very watershed of
life now and for all eternity.

Jesus was constantly confronted by religious leaders who
rejected his claims and disputed his words. On one occasion

he made a series of statements about man's deepest needs. He said, "I am the bread of life; he who comes to me shall not hunger, and he who believes in me shall never thirst" (John 6:35). He went on to say that there will be a "last day" when those who believe in him and therefore have eternal life will be raised up to be with him.

Christ's claim to have come down from heaven was challenged, and he countered by asserting the centrality of his mission—to draw men to his Father. This he followed with the astounding affirmation that his own flesh was the bread from heaven: "Unless you eat the flesh of the Son of man and drink his blood, you have no life in you; he who eats my flesh and drinks my blood has eternal life, and I will raise him up at the last day" (John 6:53, 54).

Throughout this discourse Christ spoke as God's supreme gift to man and man's only hope. The condition for man was to "believe"; the rest was an unfolding of God's love, grace, and mercy.

The result? Many of those who had been following him said, "This is a hard saying; who can listen to it?" Jesus replied, "Do you take offense at this? Then what if you were to see the Son of man ascending where he was before? It is the spirit that gives life, the flesh is of no avail; the words that I have spoken to you are spirit and life."

This was too much. "After this many of his disciples drew back and no longer went about with him."

This same state of affairs prevails in the world today. Men have rejected the divine revelation in God's creative power and wisdom. They have rejected his revelation in the person of his Son. They have rejected the revelation given in his Written Word. The results: confusion and chaos.

At this point in the story our Lord turned to the twelve he had chosen as apostles: "Will you also go away?" he asked. Simon Peter—bless his impulsive heart!—replied: "Lord, to whom shall we go? You have the words of eternal life; and we have believed, and have come to know, that you are the Holy One of God."

Confronted as we are by a world in chaos and confusion; daily encountering people who, bruised by the world and living in spiritual darkness, are as sheep without a shepherd, what shall we do?

So often we, as individual Christians and as a corporate Church, fail in our obligations to others. Our failure is a tragic reminder of our need for constant renewal in Christ.

Jesus repeatedly healed the sick. On occasion he fed the hungry. There was never any question about his love and compassion. But as one reads the total record, this stands out: he came into the world not so much to preach the Gospel as that *there might be a Gospel to preach.*

These deep truths he uttered about the bread and drink of life had to do with *eternal* life. He was speaking of the spiritual implications of his death and resurrection, and the majority of his hearers rejected his message and went their own way.

Men are no wiser today. Even in the circles of religion, many reject the clear affirmation of Jesus Christ in favor of doctrines more acceptable to human reason and philosophical presuppositions. And because they offer a lost and desperately confused world the stones of worldly wisdom and human speculation, the confusion is increased.

The Pharisees were "blind leaders of the blind" in their day, and they have their counterparts today in those whose wooden interpretations reject the spirit of Christ's message, and in those who reject the deep spiritual truths of man's lost condition and his need of redemption.

Our Lord's attitude to the Pharisees was one of ruthless denunciation for their legalism and hypocrisy. With equal forcefulness he showed the folly of the Sadducees: "You are wrong, because you know neither the scriptures nor the power of God" (Matt. 22:29).

Called to bear clear witness to a confused and lost world, we only too often add to the confusion by interposing our own opinions rather than the simple Gospel of redemption in the person and work of Jesus Christ. Little wonder that the world has turned from the Church! Little wonder the Church has lost its influence! Little wonder that we individual Christians find ourselves powerless!

Too many of us know neither the Scriptures nor the power of God. We are compromising our witness by living inconsistent lives. We are rendering our teaching and preaching void by "interpreting" away the true meaning of the Holy Scriptures, by substituting for "Thus saith the Lord" the opinions and denials of "scholars" who depend more on their "findings" and those of others like them than on what God would say to us in his Word.

Little wonder that the world is confused! Too many trumpets give an uncertain sound. Some Christians lack love and compassion, some magnify the creature more than the Creator, some are more concerned with what man thinks than with what God has clearly said.

These are stirring days, days of great opportunity and challenge. But we must remember this: the needs of the world, and of individuals, are fully met in that which Jesus Christ has done once for all. Beneath the veneer of a sophisticated and affluent man of the sixties lie the same sins of the flesh and spirit that have beset men of every generation. And it was to forgive men and cleanse them from these sins that Christ came, died, and rose again. That is the Gospel in its stark simplicity.

Why complicate what God has made so simple? Why seek

for solutions that are no solutions? Why not give God a chance in our own lives and in our witness to others—the chance to prove that faith in what he has done is the power of God for salvation to all who will believe.

With Jesus Christ one stands on an unshakable foundation. Without him there can only be confusion.

You are confused by social action. Ask . . .

WHAT IS THE GOSPEL?

The Gospel is one thing and the fruits of the Gospel are something else. They are like the roots of a vine and the grapes that grow on it.

The Gospel, the "Good News," is a message, the accepting of which produces new men with new ideals and ethics. The ideals and ethics proceeding from the Gospel are as impossible to achieve without it as are grapes without the root and vine.

Yet there is abroad today a feeling that society can be saved without the salvation of the individual. This idea is appealing because it presents man with something he can accomplish for himself and for the social order, without challenge to his personal beliefs or way of life.

The Gospel calls for the humiliation and subordination of self and the magnifying of Christ. It is a supernatural message about a supernatural person that brings about supernatural changes in the lives of those who accept it.

To a patient with diphtheria, the good news is that a cure—antitoxin—is available. When a house bursts into flame, it is good news that a fire brigade is on the way. When a car

211

engine is sputtering, it is good news that a mechanic is available.

The Gospel is the best news of all, for it is the answer to man's greatest need. It is the offer of clean hands and a pure heart for those who are defiled. It is the offer of the divine heart transplant, a new heart for the old. It promises a renewed mind, one that can grasp the things of the Spirit.

How wise we are if we face up to the depravity of the human heart! The Prophet Jeremiah says: "The heart is deceitful above all things, and desperately corrupt; who can understand it?" (Jer. 17:9).

Our Lord enumerated the wretched fruits of the unregenerate heart: "For out of the heart come evil thoughts [the natural minds of men], murder [hate], adultery [lust], fornication [uncleanness], theft [covetousness], false witness [lying], slander [vindictiveness]. These are what defile a man" (Matt. 15:19, 20a).

The Apostle Paul also describes the miserable state of the unregenerate heart in his letter to the Galatians: "Now the works of the flesh are plain: immorality, impurity, licentiousness, idolatry, sorcery, enmity, strife, jealousy, anger, selfishness, dissention, party spirit, envy, drunkenness, carousing, and the like. I warn you, as I warned you before, that those who do such things shall not inherit the kingdom of God" (Gal. 5:19–21).

Speaking in another letter as though he were talking to America in 1969, he says: "Do not be deceived; neither the immoral, nor idolaters, nor adulterers, nor homosexuals, nor thieves, nor the greedy, nor drunkards, nor revilers, nor robbers will inherit the kingdom of God" (I Cor. 6:9, 10).

Add to this dismal catalogue of the sins of the flesh the equally damning sins of pride, lovelessness, insensibility to the condition and needs of others—sins both of commission and of omission—and we find ourselves convicted in thought, word, and deed.

We all are guilty. Let's not compound our guilt by ignoring or denying the divine diagnosis. The Bible tells us, "For there is no distinction; since all have sinned and fall short of the glory of God" (Rom. 3:22b, 23), and, "Sin came into the world through one man and death through sin, and so death spread to all men because all men sinned" (Rom. 5:12).

This, then, is the miserable state of the natural man. If we are honest with ourselves we must admit it. I *know* that this was the state of my own heart and life until I accepted in faith the One who changed the entire situation for this life and for eternity. The change came when I believed God's diagnosis and accepted his cure; and the message that told me what God offered was the Gospel.

I have seen a patient indignantly reject the diagnosis of cancer, only to die miserably a few months later. Similarly, otherwise intelligent people refuse to admit God's diagnosis of sin in their lives, and through that refusal ultimately reap the certain end.

There is a growing awareness of the increased danger of cancer for cigarette smokers. The Surgeon General's office has issued a number of warnings, and now on radio and TV we hear that "it's a case of life, or breath."

What about another warning: "For the wages of sin is death"? But an alternative is given along with the warning: "The free gift of God is eternal life in Christ Jesus our Lord" (Rom. 6:23). *That is the Gospel!*

What miserable substitutes for the Gospel are being offered to hopeless sinners today! They are to be found in the teachings of cults; in vapid ethical homilies; in the words and activities of those who regard social revolution as the Gospel;

in the sermons of those who deny the content of the Gospel itself.

The Gospel is God's Good News that there is an escape from the effects of sin and its certain judgment. It is the message that the miserable wretch on skid row and the sophisticated matron in the social register are alike sinners in God's sight, with the same disease and needing the same cure. Both are offered. It tells of a restored fellowship that is sweet beyond words.

Little wonder that the Gospel is called the Good News. It is the best news in all the world, and for those who hear and believe, this news lasts for all eternity.

While the sins that plague mankind and are the cause of most newspaper headlines today are the fruit of the wickedness of the human heart, there is another kind of fruit that is found only in the lives of men and women who, by faith and the power of the Holy Spirit, have been changed (converted, born again). This fruit is beautiful to behold and comforting to experience. "The fruit of the Spirit is love, joy, peace, patience, kindness, goodness, faithfulness, gentleness, self-control; against such there is no law. And those who belong to Christ Jesus have crucified the flesh with its passions and desires" (Gal. 5:22–24). These things are *the fruits of the Gospel!*

How tragic to replace this marvelous message of hope with futile exhortations to men to lift themselves and the social order of which they are a part by some form of boot-strap endeavor! To the Church, and to individual Christians, there has been committed the preaching, teaching, and living of the gospel message.

If we give the Gospel top priority, it will change things. There is no other way to bring results that last.

There must be a difference,
for Christians set an . . .

EXAMPLE

A song popular some years ago started out, "Me and my shadow, strolling down the avenue." This points to the undeniable fact that no man can escape his own shadow.

A truth of far deeper significance that applies to all men, but particularly to Christians is that each of us casts a shadow of influence on other lives, either for good or for evil. The Psalmist expresses the gravity of this thought in a prayer, "Let not those who hope in thee be put to shame through me, O Lord God of hosts; let not those who seek thee be brought to dishonor through me, O God of Israel" (Ps. 69:6, RSV).

Our Lord himself uttered the warning: "Temptations to sin are sure to come; but woe to him by whom they come! It would be better for him if a millstone were hung around his neck and he were cast into the sea, than that he should cause one of these little ones to sin" (Luke 17:1, 2).

Christians can be woefully careless in this matter of example and by their carelessness contribute to the downfall of others.

The believers in Corinth were confronted with the problem of pagan rites involving the placing of food before idols. This food was then often sold in the market, and a controversy soon arose over whether Christians should buy or eat such meat. Paul went on to tell them that eating meat had no significance one way or the other, but that the effect of a careless attitude could be disastrous for a weak Christian. He concluded, "Therefore, if food is a cause of my brother's falling, I will never eat meat, lest I cause my brother to fall" (I Cor. 8:13).

How many today are willing to take Paul's position? I fear that many of us, convinced of our own freedom and of the rightness of our behavior within that freedom, forget that "none of us lives to himself, and none of us dies to himself" (Rom. 14:7). We live in the presence of God, who sees and knows all. We also have about us a host of persons—some of whom we do not even know, perhaps—who look to us to set an example.

Paul speaks of this in forceful terms: "Then let us no more pass judgment on one another, but rather decide never to put a stumbling-block or hindrance in the way of a brother. . . . Do not let what you eat cause the ruin of one for whom Christ died. . . . Do not, for the sake of food, destroy the work of God. . . . Happy is he who has no reason to judge himself for what he approves" (Rom. 14:13, 15, 20, 22).

For us to set some sort of example is as inevitable as for light to produce a shadow. A good example is a reflection of the indwelling Christ. A good example glorifies Christ; a bad one shows the triumph of self (and Satan) in our lives.

Furthermore, the Christian's example has both a positive and a negative aspect, produced by what we do and by what we do not do, by what we say and by what we refrain from saying.

Sinful acts can "cause the enemies of the Lord to blaspheme," as David's adultery did. How tragic when those who bear the name Christian are guilty of thus demeaning the name of Christ and hindering his cause. The Christian's outward behavior should reflect resources beyond himself, and standards pleasing to God rather than the world.

Few would deny that the growth of juvenile delinquency in our day is mainly due to the bad example, in word and deed, set by so many adults. Christians are not without blame. Often they so conform their behavior to that of the world that it can be said that their salt has lost its savor and their light its power.

Setting a bad example by carelessness or thoughtlessness is common, even among Christians. Questionable jokes that suggest some uncleanness, witty remarks that show an irreverent attitude, careless behavior that implies evil—all these things take their toll of our moral influence. Paul's admonition, "Do not be conformed to this world but be transformed by the renewal of your mind" (Rom. 12:2a) bears directly on the example the Christian sets before others.

How easy, too, to harm our influence by fits of temper, hasty words, unworthy deeds! All about us unbelievers are walking in spiritual darkness. It is tragic indeed when Christians, who should reflect the light of the living Christ to all around, only deepen the darkness by careless behavior that hides the light of Christ within. Many unbelievers have no interest in the doctrines or principles of Christianity, but they are uncomfortably keen-sighted about the practices of professing Christians.

The answer to the question of our example to others is not to be found in some pietistic set of rules. It is a matter of living in the conscious presence of the Lord, trying to please him in word, thought, and deed. This inevitably reflects itself in our example to others. The Apostle Paul advises, "Abstain from all appearances of evil" (I Thess. 5:22, KJV). This

217

means simply: if there is a question or even a suggestion of evil, *avoid it.*

This is *not* negative Christianity. A Christian should certainly live a life consistent with his profession. Inevitably some will sneer, and occasionally some will persecute. One of our privileges as Christians is to accept the offense of the Cross.

No man ever set a more consistent example of righteousness than the Prophet Daniel. When a plot was hatched to discredit him with the king, his enemies said, "We shall not find any ground for complaint against this Daniel unless we find it in connection with the law of his God" (Dan. 6:5). Then, when it was decreed that for thirty days no petition was to be made to anyone other than the king, Daniel went to his house and "prayed and gave thanks before God, as he had done previously" (Dan. 5:10*b*). This he did three times a day before an open window, knowing that his enemies would see and accuse him. What an example to all who would be faithful to the heavenly vision, regardless of the apparent consequences!

It has been said that people judge far more by what they see than what they hear. Certainly the influence of the Christian rests in large measure on his behavior. Pious words may come easy, but true Christian character produces upright living that people see. Such an example brings glory to God.

Christian character, the source of a good example, is a matter of day-to-day living, judging things and events in the light of God's laws and holiness and patterning one's behavior accordingly. It involves looking beyond the immediate to the eternal, but with the realization that those around us are also looking—not at God, but at the things in us that either honor or dishonor him.

Only as Christ lives in us can we be a good influence. The shadow of our example falls behind us, affecting for good or ill all touched by it.

For good or for ill? That is the question.

Be careful, for today all around us we see . . .

THE DEMON OF LUST

There are millions of demon-possessed people in the United States—possessed by the unclean spirit of lust.

Satan, the prince of this world, fans the flames of lust in the hearts of men and women. Playing on one of the strongest urges of nature—one that, when controlled, is one of God's great gifts to mankind—Satan has down through the ages perverted it, wherever he can, for the destruction of his victims.

Some may think it fantastic to say that lust is a demon, but let them not forget that there is perhaps no more vulnerable point in the human personality, and that sex obsession has been a prime reason for personal and national disintegration all through human history.

America seems to have gone nearly to the limit in worship at the shrine of sex. In every medium of communication today, authors, publishers, producers, and advertisers vie with one another in encouraging lust.

History is filled with records of religions that have fostered unbridled lust, some through phallic objects of worship, others by the use of cult prostitutes. But not until the last few years has the Christian Church been infiltrated by those who have regarded the Seventh Commandment as relative. Through the permissiveness and twisted philosophy of the "new morality" and "situation ethics," these persons have attempted to break down the moral concepts and restraints of God's holy laws. Our risen Lord's denunciation of those in the church at Pergamum who "taught" men to "commit fornication" (Rev. 2:14) is going unheeded by these new apostles of "freedom," with devastating results to themselves and to their victims— usually young people.

Perhaps only those from whom this demon has been exorcised can tell the sordid story of lives so possessed. Like David of old they can rejoice: "He brought me up out of an horrible pit, out of the miry clay, and set my feet upon a rock, and established my goings" (Ps. 40:2).

The points of entrance of this demon are legion. Usually he finds easy access through the thoughts. Like bottle flies swarming over a carcass, thoughts flit hither and yon and linger on forbidden areas and uncleanness until the soul is saturated with filth.

The lustful look—how easy to let the eye linger even as the mind gloats. Who can withstand such temptations? Who can say, I am not guilty? The Apostle James describes the process of this demon's work: "Every man is tempted when he is drawn away of his own lust, and enticed. Then when lust hath conceived, it bringeth forth sin: and sin, when it is finished, bringeth forth death" (Jas. 1:14, 15).

The lustful thoughts, the lustful looks lead on to the lustful acts—and without the forgiving and cleansing power of the Saviour, these lead on to death.

Many of today's novels, particularly paperbacks, are wholly unrestrained in describing any and every kind of lewdness and perversion. And for a play or movie to become a hit now, it seems almost essential (so the producers say) to portray some form of sexual activity—even perversion. Those who feed their minds on this garbage find themselves possessed by the demon of lust, with an insatiable desire for more and more filth.

Newspapers and magazines often warn of the dangers of mixing alcohol and driving, of the immediate and ultimate dangers of LSD and other hallucinatory drugs, and of other things that are a menace to health. But only the Church has the message about the things that harm the *soul*, and of late the Church has been woefully silent about those moral standards affirmed by Christ and his Word. The demon of lust is unrecognized. The Church seems more concerned with social problems—few of which have eternal implications.

Lust defiles the mind, body, and spirit; it consumes its victims with unholy desire. The writer of the Epistle to the Hebrews speaks clearly: "God will judge the immoral and adulterous." The risen and triumphant Son of God pronounces solemn judgment on the "polluted" and fornicators: they are among those whose "lot shall be in the lake that burns with fire and brimstone, which is the second death" (Rev. 21:8). The Apostle Paul is equally explicit: "Be sure of this, that no immoral or impure man has any inheritance in the kingdom of Christ and of God" (Eph. 5:5).

Has God set for mankind standards that cannot be met? Humanly speaking, he has. The natural man finds himself bound in the chains of the flesh. But right at this point there lies the wonder of the Gospel: What we cannot do, Christ does for us. The temptations that constantly assail us are never greater than we can bear, by his grace and strength. The demon of lust can be exorcised. This Christ will do for all who turn to him for help.

Perhaps at no point is the compassion of our Lord more

in evidence. He forgave the woman taken in adultery even as her accusers slunk away, convicted by their own consciences. Denouncing the Pharisees for their hypocrisy Jesus said, "The tax collectors and the harlots go into the kingdom of God before you . . . , [for] the tax collectors and harlots believed him—[John the Baptist]; and even when you saw it, you did not afterward repent and believe him" (Matt. 21:31*b*, 32*b*).

There is victory over the demon of lust, victory by the Cross. Christ died to condemn sin in the flesh and to give freedom and release to those who look to him.

These are days of unusual testing. The demons of lust lurk on every hand. Like David of old all of us can say, "As the Lord lives . . . there is but a step between me and death." Satan controls so many areas of life that we are confronted by these temptations daily.

But God offers to give us clean hands and a pure heart, by an act of creation. After his double sin of adultery and murder, David prayed, "Create in me a clean heart" (Ps. 51:10).

Beware of self-reformation! The demon may depart only to return with others. This must be a work of God's grace—a cleansing by the atoning blood of the Cross and an infilling with his Spirit.

We must have help . . .

WHERE THE NEED IS

A favorite phrase of the day is, "Where the action is." Some people and places appeal to many because they are centers of activity.

The constant source of comfort and joy for the Christian is that Jesus Christ is always found where the need is, and that he makes full provision for that need.

At the very beginning let us make clear the distinction between "using God" for our own purposes—a reflection on our concept of God and of Christianity—and appropriating the things God has made available for those who trust in him.

If a person in need refused to make use of something that was his for the taking and that would meet his need, he would seem foolish, to say the least.

While the world has no right to demand for itself blessings that accrue only to believers, Christians owe it to themselves to appropriate all that they have in Christ. No Christian, having received by faith forgiveness of sins and the redemption offered in the Gospel, should continue to live as a spiritual beggar.

First of all, we need *daily cleansing*. The world tarnishes, the flesh besmirches. On every hand we are confronted by the allurements of Satan. Sometimes we succumb, and the result is a soiling no earthly detergent can remove. Day by day we need cleansing and forgiveness, a renewing of spiritual concepts and perspectives. All this is available through the Holy Spirit.

There is not a day that we do not also need *guidance* to lead us out of uncertainty. The promises for such help are found all through the Bible. For example: "In all your ways acknowledge him, and he will make straight your paths" (Prov. 3:6, RSV). And from James: "If any of you lacks wisdom, let him ask God who gives to all men generously and without reproaching, and it will be given him" (1:5).

Besides cleansing and guidance, God offers the Christian help for specific problems. *Impatience!* How common, and how detrimental to the Christian's witness! God supplies serenity in the midst of pressures, quietness in turmoil, to those who seek it. For the Christian, the meaning of the phrase "inner resources" should be experienced and exhibited.

Who has not experienced an overwhelming sense of *weakness* when confronted by the many temptations and problems which are a part of living in the world? God supplies strength to those who are weak. Realizing this, the Apostle Paul was able to make the paradoxical statement: "For the sake of Christ, then, I am content with weaknesses, insults, hardships, persecutions, and calamities; for when I am weak, then I am strong" (II Cor. 12:10).

Few indeed are the Christians who do not have a *lack of genuine love* for others. This lovelessness has one cure, an infilling of the Holy Spirit, who brings love. It is a discredit to Christians that so few obey the Lord's command: "This I command you, to love one another" (John 15:17). He will supply this love that we need.

Never in the history of the world have people been subjected to such *tensions* as they are today in this contracted, complicated society. What a glorious opportunity for Christians to demonstrate quietness of spirit and of heart! But this is not something we contrive for ourselves. Rather, it is a blessing God grants when we rest in him and avail ourselves of such promises as, "Thou dost keep him in perfect peace, whose mind is stayed on thee, because he trusts in thee" (Isa. 26:3); or, "In peace I will both lie down and sleep; for thou alone, O Lord, makest me dwell in safety" (Ps. 4:8). Idealistic? Theoretical? Impractical? Try it and see!

For some, *doubt* is a problem. Satan raises questions about the validity of faith, through a book, perhaps, or a conversation, or a sermon. However it happens, the experience is disturbing; but our Lord is very willing to settle it for us. Faith is the answer to doubt. To those who are willing to receive it, God gives the assurance of the reality of himself and his promises. Faith should be so firm that with the Apostle Paul we can say, "What if some were unfaithful? Does their faithlessness nullify the faithfulness of God? By no means! Let God be true though every man be false, as it is written, 'That thou mayest be justified in thy words, and prevail when thou art judged'" (Rom. 3:3, 4).

When one has caught a vision of the reality of God and the finality of his revelation, faith rests in him regardless of what may happen.

Often going hand in hand with doubt is *discouragement*. Thank God for the words of encouragement in his Word. God is sovereign, faithful, able, willing. We have only to appropriate what he has provided for us, and our discouragement will be replaced by a renewed joy as we realize the truth of Paul's affirmation: "What then shall we say to this? If God is for us, who is against us? He who did not spare his own Son but gave him up for us all, will he not also give us all things with him?" (Rom. 8:31, 32).

Nowhere is our need more evident than in the *temptations* that confront us continually. And for this need also God has a clear answer: "No temptation has overtaken you that is not common to man. God is faithful, and he will not let you be tempted beyond your strength, but with the temptation will also provide the way of escape, that you may be able to endure it" (I Cor. 10:13). How it helps to realize that our Lord "was tempted in all points like as we are, yet without sin"! He knows. He understands. He delivers.

Sorrow is a part of this life. At times it can become so overwhelming that life hardly seems worth living. But for sorrow the Lord offers comfort; for mourning he gives joy. There may be sorrow for sins, which should bring repentance. There may be sorrow over personal loss or over the actions of others. But there is no sorrow that a loving Lord cannot heal.

Some suffer from a sense of *inadequacy*. This is a psychological matter that can be met in the presence of our Lord. Paul spoke to this problem when he said that we are not "sufficient of ourselves to claim anything as coming from us; our sufficiency is from God" (II Cor. 3:5). A feeling of our own adequacy is dangerous. But when we realize the complete adequacy of our God and put our faith in him, what a difference, and what a sense of his overwhelming power!

How often we go down in *defeat* before the enemy of souls. Yet how wonderful that defeat can be changed into victory. The words of the old hymn, "Each victory will help you some other to win," can prove a reality. We all are in a

227

continuing battle, but the victory is assured if we use the resources God offers.

God's provisions are to be found at the point of the believer's need. There is no circumstance for which he has not provided.

Some may be eager to be "where the action is." Christians have the privilege of being where the needs are met.

Confused? Discouraged? the Bible
tells us that the
return of Christ is the blessed . . .

HOPE

A serious accident has taken place and a loved one, unconscious and bleeding, is rushed to the hospital and taken immediately to the operating room. After what seems like hours of agonized waiting the surgeon comes out, and you immediately ask the questions uppermost in your heart: "How is he?" "Is there hope?"

If the surgeon smiles as he comes to you and says, "Don't worry; he'll be all right," what a relief! What a surge of joy and thankfulness!

As the word and assurance of the surgeon bring hope for the recovery of the injured one, so the Christian faith gives hope for eternity. Christianity is the religion of hope. Christ is the door of hope. To his bewildered and apprehensive disciples of an earlier day he spoke the word of hope; "I will come again and will take you to myself, that where I am you may be also" (John 14:3*b*); and to his own of this generation he gives the same promise. But for some the time seems very long, the way very rough.

I have crossed the Pacific by boat several times. On every trip there were days of calm seas and clear skies. But some times the waves were high, and on occasion storms seemed to threaten the safety of the ship. Day after day we proceeded on course, with the horizons ever unattainably merging into new ones.

But inevitably the time came when a thrill of excitement ran through the passengers. Land had been sighted, and before long we would be safely in the harbor. All the time the captain and crew had known that beyond the horizon there was land and the desired haven, and the passengers had, by faith, shared in this hope. We read of our heavenly hope in the Book of Hebrews: "So that . . . we who have fled for refuge might have strong encouragement to seize the hope set before us. We have this as a sure and steadfast anchor of the soul, a hope that enters into the inner shrine behind the curtain, where Jesus has gone as a forerunner on our behalf" (Heb. 6:18–20a).

What a glorious hope! The anchor of our souls safely fixed in the harbor, unseen but sure because Jesus himself has gone ahead for us.

In contrast, how vast is the hopelessness of the unbeliever! The Apostle Paul wrote the Christians in Ephesus: "Remember that you were . . . separated from Christ, alienated from the commonwealth of Israel, and strangers to the covenants of promise, having no hope and without God in the world" (Eph. 2:12). These same people, once hopeless, had found their hope in the One who died for them, so that Paul could say, "In him you also, who have heard the word of truth, the gospel of your salvation, and have believed in him, were sealed with the promised Holy Spirit, which is the guarantee of our inheritance until we acquire possession of it, to the praise of his glory" (Eph. 1:13, 14).

Today there is a grave danger in the organized church of dispensing entirely with the element of eternal hope by substituting humanism for Christianity, with a one-sided emphasis on man's physical welfare and economic security. Important as these latter things are, they must not be given priority over the soul's welfare and the eternal verities. Paul warns, "If in this life only we have hope in Christ, we are of all men most miserable" (I Cor. 15:19, KJV).

Some years ago a man was crossing New York harbor on a ferry and, being interested in machinery, went down into the engine room. Everything was spotless, and the brass shone like a mirror. When he complimented the engineer for this, the engineer replied with a shining face, "I have a glory in my heart." How few of us reflect the hope and glory of belonging to Christ by the way we look and the work we do!

There are many facets of Christian hope. In Hebrews it is spoken of variously as a "homeland," "a better country," a "heavenly" one, a city "God has prepared," "a kingdom that cannot be shaken," an "everlasting city," "the city which is to come." And Jesus implies that ours is a heavenly citizenship in the words, "They are not of the world, even as I am not of the world" (John 17:16).

The Christian's hope, far from excluding concern and compassion for the less fortunate, should produce not only love for his fellow men and concern for their material needs but also a strong desire that they might share the same precious hope that is his in Christ.

This hope rests on the sure foundation of the revelation God has given of his truth, his promises that cannot fail, his faithfulness and ability to fulfill what he has promised—all secured through the person and work of Jesus Christ.

It is a hope sustained by the faith that is "the assurance of things hoped for, the conviction of things not seen" (Heb. 11:1). It rests with an unswerving confidence in the fact that Christ has secured our future and that day by day *all things* are being fitted together for our good by a loving and sovereign God.

The Christian's hope is nourished by the Scriptures. There he finds his faith strengthened by the assurance that "whatsoever was written in former days was written for our instruction, that by steadfastness and by the encouragement of the scriptures we might have hope" (Rom. 15:4). He is almost intoxicated with a godly optimism. Like David he can say, "Even though I walk through the valley of the shadow of death, I fear no evil" (Ps. 23:4a).

By the Scriptures he is brought into a full assurance, so that he can say with Paul that he *knows* the Christ revealed there through personal experience and knows that Christ is able to keep everything committed to him "against that day."

This hope also involves an expectation of the Lord's return: "For the grace of God has appeared for the salvation of all men, training us to renounce irreligion and worldly passions, and to live sober, upright, and godly lives in this world, awaiting our blessed hope, the appearing of the glory of our great God and Savior Jesus Christ" (Titus 2:11–13).

This hope that sustained the early Christians is still our shining prospect. We *know* a better day is coming, a glorious day when Christ shall return, "coming on the clouds of heaven with power and great glory" (Matt. 24:30b).

Finally, the facts about our hope should be transmitted to our children—"that the next generation might know them, the children yet unborn, and arise and tell them to their children, so that they should set their hope in God, and not forget the works of God, but keep his commandments" (Ps. 78:6, 7).

How we of this generation are failing in this duty to our children! Little wonder that many are in revolt, disillusioned but desperately poor spiritually—all because they see no good end for the world. Much that we see in young people today stems from an utter hopelessness. They see so little in many Christians to commend the Gospel they profess.

Christianity is the religion of hope, and a joy to experience —for we belong to the Creator-Redeemer, the King of kings and the Lord of lords, now and forever.

But, we must be . . .

HONEST WITH GOD

It is not easy to be honest with God. Rarely do any of us face up to actualities when we pray. But whom do we think we are fooling? Either we think God is very obtuse or else we presume upon his grace and mercy and salve our consciences with the feeling that he does not know or does not care.

We may try to sweep our sins under the rug, assume a hypocritical air of innocence, and go our own willful way. But God sees no rug, only the unconfessed and unrepented sins that form a barrier between us and him. These sins may be sins of the spirit (such as unbelief, pride, jealousy, envy, censoriousness) or of the flesh (such as lust, intemperance, love of money, dishonesty).

Failure to be honest with God is a continuing source of unhappiness, frustration, and ineffectiveness as Christians. On the other hand, complete honesty in confessing all sins, whether they be of thought, word, or deed, brings peace of mind and spirit and is the first step to a life of usefulness as a Christian.

Psalm 139 tells us that God knows our every thought and motive. "Even before a word is on my tongue, lo, O LORD,

234

thou knowest it altogether" (v. 4, RSV). There is no place to which we can flee and escape God. The darkness cannot cover us: "even darkness is not dark to thee, the night is as bright as the day; for darkness is as light with thee" (v. 12).

Little wonder that David ends this psalm, "Search me, O God, and know my heart! Try me and know my thoughts! And see if there be any wicked way in me, and lead me in the way everlasting!" (vv. 23, 24).

Our unwillingness to be honest with God may stem from our failure to realize his all-seeing eye. "Before him no creature is hidden, but all are open and laid bare to the eyes of him with whom we have to do" (Heb. 4:13). Is this a frightening thought? Far from it. It is comforting to know that God, who knows and sees into the depths of our hearts, sees our feeble aspirations for righteousness and meets them with his own loving concern and help.

David knew well the difference between being honest with God and trying to hide his sins. When he prayed, "Clear thou me from hidden faults" (Ps. 19:12b), he was admitting the tendency to think that things done in secret are unknown to God. In Psalm 32 he tells of the anguish of soul he suffered when he did not confess his sins and the joy and peace that came with honest confession.

What we are in our hearts God already knows. Why foolishly pretend that we are something else? We often deceive others, but we can never deceive God.

How are we dishonest with God?

Think about our prayers. When we pray, "Forgive our sins," do we not hasten by or gloss over that lustful thought and pretend it has escaped God's notice? Do we not conveniently ignore the dishonest act, the "cutting of a corner" in a business deal, rather than explicitly confessing it? Often we harbor envy or jealousy against someone; do we confess these specific sins?

There can be no honesty with God without confession and repentance. Because these essentials are evaded, individual Christians and the Church are weak.

There can be no power in prayer if between us and God there stands unconfessed sin. "If I had cherished iniquity in my heart, the Lord would not have listened" (Ps. 66:18). The confession of guilt is the door to forgiveness. Repentance is the sure way to be heard.

We are also not honest with God until we are willing to submit to his will in every area of our lives. Christ did not come to redeem us so that we should live thereafter according to our own desires. The Bible makes it abundantly clear that God wants the best for his children and that the best is found only in conformity to his will. There is no honesty in thinking we can hold to God with one hand while we cling to the world with the other. Honesty demands that we obey him in every plan and in every part of our lives.

We are not honest with God until we admit the enormity of our own sinfulness—confessed to him in detail—and the enormity of his love, mercy, and forgiveness in Christ.

To presume upon the grace and mercy of God without confessing and repenting only adds to our sins. The Apostle Jude speaks of "ungodly persons who pervert the grace of our God into licentiousness" (Jude 4b), while Paul speaks of the idea of sinning that grace may abound as a "ghastly thought" (Phillips). Are not most of us guilty of claiming mercy and forgiveness without giving honest thought to open and full confession?

Honesty with God is both intellectual and emotional. It demands truthfulness in our estimate of ourselves, a recognition of the nature of sin and its many manifestations in our own hearts. David says, "Behold, thou desirest truth in the inward being; therefore teach me wisdom in my secret heart," and, "The sacrifice acceptable to God is a broken spirit; a

broken and contrite heart, O God, thou wilt not despise"
(Ps. 51:6, 17).

God, the One who is Creator and Preserver of life, the
One who is omnipotent, omniscient, and omnipresent, the
One who is altogether holy and sovereign, is full of love,
mercy, and compassion. Honesty demands that we come to
him in humility and contrition, hiding nothing, confessing all.
In this way we receive the pardon, blessings, and fellowship
he is so anxious to give. To approach him in any other way
is sheer presumption. To think we can hide anything from
him or evade the truth before him is folly.

The Prophet Jeremiah was honest with both God and
man. Today we should heed his words: "Thus says the LORD:
'Let not the wise man glory in his wisdom, let not the
mighty man glory in his might, let not the rich man glory
in his riches; but let him who glories glory in this, that
he understands and knows me, that I am the LORD who
practices kindness, justice, and righteousness in the earth;
for in these things I delight, says the LORD'" (Jer. 9:23, 24).

The Apostle Paul was equally honest with God. In all his
letters, one senses his unswerving determination to see himself and the world around him in the light of God's revealed
truth, and because of this he speaks to us today. Aware of
his past, he spoke of himself as the chief of sinners. Aware of
God's redemptive work in his own heart, he could speak of
being crucified with Christ. Such honesty has its great reward
—complete surrender to and identification with the living
Saviour.

As I search my own heart, I realize how often I have failed
to be honest with God. And I know such failure stifles my
Christian life at the very point where it should be strengthened.

How absurd it is to think we have deceived the One from whom nothing can be hid. The best way to change is to start being honest. Hide nothing from God, and you will find a joy and peace that can come in no other way.

In every battle . . .

RECOGNIZE YOUR ENEMY

Many people are unaware that we live in enemy-occupied territory. As a result, they are often booby-trapped and fooled into making all kinds of disastrous mistakes.

Dr. Emile Caillet has expressed the danger in these words: "One of the neatest tricks Satan has ever performed is to convince so many people that he does not exist." How true! And how many there are who go down to defeat because they do not know the enemy and how he works!

In his *Mere Christianity*, C. S. Lewis pointed out: "Christianity agrees with Dualism that this universe is at war. But it does not think this is a war between independent powers. It thinks it is a civil war, a rebellion, and that we are living in a part of the universe occupied by the rebel.

"Enemy-occupied territory—that is what this world is. Christianity is the story of how the rightful king has landed, you might say landed in disguise, and is calling us all to take part in a great campaign of sabotage. . . . I know someone will ask me, 'Do you really mean, at this time of day, to reintroduce our old friend the devil—hoofs and horns and all?' Well, what the time of day has to do with it I do not know. And I am not particular about the hoofs and horns. But in other respects my answer is, 'Yes, I do.' I do not claim to know anything about his personal appearance. If anybody really wants to know him better I would say to that person, 'Don't worry. If you really want to, you will. Whether you'll like it when you do is another question' " (*Mere Christianity*, Macmillan, 1960, pp. 35, 36).

The fact is that from the very beginning of Genesis to the end of the Revelation, the Bible makes repeated references to Satan, clearly stating that he is a person—evil, malignant, and persistent—but that though he is extremely active now, his doom is sealed.

The names by which he is characterized in the Scriptures speak volumes, not only about who he is but also about what he does. He is called the accuser, the adversary, the angel of the bottomless pit, the devil, the enemy, an evil spirit, a liar and the father of lies, a lying spirit, a murderer, the power of darkness, the prince of this world, the prince of the power of the air, the serpent, the spirit that worketh in the children of disobedience, the tempter, the god of this world, an unclean spirit, the wicked one, and a roaring lion.

In the light of this revelation of the nature of Satan, what folly to deny his existence or belittle his power! Were it not for the fact that his ultimate defeat was accomplished at the Cross, that he cannot stand against the Word of God, the Sword of the Spirit, and that God has provided an invincible armor for me as a Christian, I would not dare to write this article.

We sing, "This is my Father's world," and it is, by creation; but for the moment there is a usurper on the throne, the "god of this world"—the devil. We are living in "enemy territory."

Satan is doubly dangerous because he is the master of

camouflage, even appearing as an "angel of light" to deceive the unwary. There are people and institutions today that are Satan's servants, even as there were in the days of the Apostle Paul, who said of them: "For many, of whom I have often told you and now tell you even with tears, live as enemies of the cross of Christ. Their end is destruction, their god is the belly, and they glory in their shame, with minds set on earthly things" (Phil. 3:18, 19). Think of the danger for those who do not recognize the enemy and his work!

How can we tell? How can we know whether something is of God or of the deceiver? A Christian is given something like a spiritual mine detector. He is instructed to ask when in doubt: Does it honor God? Does it glorify his Son? Is it true to his written Word? Does it give evidence of the presence and blessing of the Holy Spirit?

As the committed Christian finds himself confronted with Satan's counterfeits, the Holy Spirit warns: Be careful! Wait! This does not conform to God's revealed truth!

Jesus repeatedly warned against the works of Satan. He said that it is the evil one who snatches the seed of the Gospel from the hearts of the ignorant and indifferent. Speaking of the weeds growing where good seed had been sown, he said, "An enemy has done this." And at this point he gave a warning many ignore today, a specific warning against "weed-pulling," because the wheat is pulled up with the weeds. Jesus' word is, "Let them grow together until the harvest; and at harvest time I will tell the reapers, Gather the weeds first and bind them in bundles to be burned, but gather the wheat into my barn" (Matt. 13:30)—small comfort to Satan and his dupes, and a warning to overzealous Christians.

Today, as always, Satan works to disrupt and destroy. The Apostle Paul, writing to the church in Corinth, says about the devil, "we are not ignorant of his devices." We know his devices are legion.

Wherever the blight of Communism falls, the Church and Christians are sure to come under attack. Twenty-five years ago there were 8,000 Protestant missionaries in China. To-day there is not one. Twenty-five years ago there were 275 Christian hospitals in China. Today not one is left. Eighteen years ago the most thriving church to be found on any mission field was in North Korea. Today every vestige of Christianity has been wiped out.

But Satan is also working his devious methods in the West. Secularism dominates most of the colleges and universities once founded by the churches. Materialism determines the goals of many men and nations. Entertainment and art worship the god of sex and lust. The reason is easy to find: "The whole world is in the power of the evil one" (I John 5:19b).

For all of this, thank God, there is an answer. There can be victory and safety. Because of the works of Satan, there is the Cross. Because of him, there is the Gospel of Christ's redemption. Because of him, we have power through the Spirit. Because of him, God prepared his own protective armor for the Christian (Eph. 6:10–18).

Man inevitably fails when he trusts himself. It is through Christ alone, "who loved us," that we are more than conquerors. And we are given one weapon with which to carry on an offensive warfare against the devil: "the sword of the Spirit, which is the word of God." Our Lord gave a perfect example of its use when he was tempted in the wilderness. Satan has never yet been able to stand against it.

Let no man deceive you—Satan is *real*. On every hand we see the evidences of his presence and work. Just as hunters follow a trail, certain that there is a cause for its existence, so we can trace the trail of Satan throughout the world, both Communist and free. It is folly to ignore him and even greater folly to ignore the One who has conquered him. Satan's end is sure: "For all that is in the world, the lust of the flesh and the lust of the eyes and the pride of life, is not of the Father but is of the world. And the world passes away, and the lust of it; but he who does the will of God abides for ever" (I John 2:16, 17).

And Remember . . .

HE STILL KNOCKS AT YOUR DOOR

The evening shadows lengthened into night as a group of neighborhood children played together on the lawn. Bushes here and there made perfect hiding places, and the shrill voices of boys and girls gave evidence of carefree childhood, unaffected by responsibilities and unaware of a restless world about them.

An old man walked by and stopped to watch the children at play. A little boy was hiding behind some shrubbery close by the fence, and to him the old man said, "Sonny, my car broke down and I had to leave it at the garage down the street. Can you tell me where there is a place I can spend the night?"

The boy turned and looked at the shadowy figure outside and replied, "Naw, I can't. Run along. I'm busy."

A crowd of teen-agers were out together. First a movie, then a stop for a Coke and dancing to a jukebox.

Crowding into their cars to continue the party in the basement recreation room of Dick's home, they hurried by a boy walking manfully down the street with the aid of leg braces and two crutches. They all knew him, but his handicap kept him from joining in their fun. Only in his studies did he excel all the rest of them.

After the cars had started one boy remarked, "We should have asked Mark to ride. It must be pretty tough carrying yourself down the street with nothing much but your shoulder muscles." "Aw, he's all right. He's used to it, and besides we haven't got room in the car," was the reply.

Across the town, students in the state university were busy preparing for exams. Many were affluent by the standards of the rest of the world; many were content with just getting by; all were enmeshed in the grind to cram enough information to graduate, in the hope of getting a good job one day.

There came a knock at the door of a room where two boys were slouched deep in chairs reading, and together they called, "Come in." The door opened and a quiet fellow neither knew very well, though they knew some of the fellows spoke of him as a "holy Joe," walked in. "I just wanted to invite you fellows to come over to the 'Y' tomorrow night to hear Dr. Ivan Cushman. He's one of the world's leading archaeologists, and he takes the Bible and makes it come alive in his lectures."

"Who wants to hear an old gravedigger anyway?" asked Jim, with little politeness to their visitor. "And who wants to hear anybody stupid enough to believe the Bible?" Chuck chimed in. "Besides, we've got an astrophysics test day after tomorrow, and that's all that counts. Toddle on and get some weaker minds to go with you."

A beautiful woman, wife of a prosperous executive, was arranging the flowers in her home for guests who were coming for dinner—one couple particularly important because his influence could mean a large government contract for her husband's firm.

The maid announced the guests, and in a few minutes gay laughter filled the air as cocktails were served and men and women mingled in the relaxed anticipation of good food and exciting companionship.

During the beautifully prepared and served dinner, a maid came to the hostess, leaned low, and whispered something in her ear. A shadow of annoyance crossed her face as she replied, "Tell them to ask someone else. This is no time to interrupt me. They should know that we have guests for dinner."

The evening passed with laughter (some jokes few would have repeated in a mixed group a few years before), and with a friendly hand of bridge followed by final drinks before the friends left.

As they were preparing to retire, the executive asked, "Jane, what was the maid whispering to you about during dinner?" His wife replied petulantly, "Oh, those Smiths down the road had a sick baby they wanted to take to the hospital. It was too far for a taxi and the buses only run every hour. They asked if someone here could drive them in one of our cars. They should have seen that we were entertaining guests."

A week passed. The midnight broadcast was about to begin, and across the city radios were turned on. Into homes and bars, cars and nightclubs, mansions and slums, there came these words of the first Advent: "And she brought forth her firstborn son, and wrapped him in swaddling clothes, and laid him in a manger; because there was no room for them in the inn."

A little boy in troubled sleep thought of an old man he had rudely told to "run along" because he was busy playing.

246

Some teen-agers who only a few minutes before had been gaily dancing to loud music suddenly remembered Mark shuffling down the street on his crutches and wished they had made room for him in their cars.

Two university students home for Christmas vacation paused to wonder whether they should have been too busy even to listen to a famous man who believed God and the Bible.

The executive looked at his wife, and she returned the uneasy stare. Had their guests been so important that they could not have spared a little time to help some poor neighbors, desperate because of a sick child?

"No room in the inn." These haunting words carried their meaning to many people in many places.

No room for Christ? No time for him! No concern for things of the spirit! No love and compassion for needy people right at their side!

The broadcast concluded with these words: "How like the people of Bethlehem are many of us tonight! No room for the Christ child! But he is no longer a child. He grew to manhood and died on a cross for the sins of the world, and he arose from the dead—and he is coming again. He speaks to us: 'Verily I say unto you, Inasmuch as ye did it not to one of the least of these, ye did it not to me.'"

In the dim recesses of many minds there came back these words: "Behold, I stand at the door and knock: if any man hear my voice, and open the door, I will come in to him, and will sup with him, and he with me."